VERMONT RECOLLECTIONS:

SIFTING MEMORIES THROUGH THE INTERVIEW PROCESS

Edited by: Jane C. Beck

#3392 1186

NORTHEAST FOLKLORE

Volume XXX   1995*

Published annually by The Maine Folklife Center, Department of
Anthropology, 5773 South Stevens Hall, University of Maine, Orono,
Maine.

Edward D. Ives, Editor
Pauleena M. MacDougall, Managing Editor

Printed by
University of Maine Printing Services
Orono, Maine
1995

The Maine Folklife Center is a non-profit organization devoted
to the collection, preservation, study and publication of the songs,
legends, tales and other traditions of New England and the Atlantic
Provinces of Canada. Regular annual membership is $25.00 per year.
All members receive the Maine Folklife Center Newsletter as it appears
and a subscription to *Northeast Folklore,* as well as a ten percent discount
on tapes, books and videos as a privilege of membership.

Northeast Folklore is an annual publication issued by the Maine
Folklife Center, formerly the Northeast Folklore Society. Each year we
hope to publish a single fresh collection of regional material or a
comparative study, but we do not rule out the possibility of making a
single volume out of several shorter collections or studies. Authors are
invited to submit manuscripts for consideration to The Editor, *Northeast
Folklore*, South Stevens Hall, University of Maine, Orono, Maine 04469.

ISBN 0-943197-22-8

* Volume XXIX was dated 1990. No volumes were issued 1991-1994.

CONTENTS

Cover Photograph: John Lamberton in his shop.
See "Keep the Saw Cutting" by Jane Beck.

ACKNOWLEDGEMENTS

My thanks go to my co-contributors for their help in preparation of this manuscript and for reading different versions of the Introduction. I would also like to thank Tim Newcomb for his detailing of various places mentioned in the manuscript and for Terri Jackman's efforts to put everything into a standard format on disk and for preparing the hard copy.

—JCB

Towns Referred to in the Interviews

INTRODUCTION

Sometime in 1989 Sandy Ives approached me about the possibility of doing a volume for *Northeast Folklore* on Vermont. I told him that there were a number of people who had been involved in collecting and editing oral histories in the state, and would it be possible to include a number of such pieces, as I felt a compendium would give a broader range and better feel for the kind of material that was here. He said that sounded like a good idea—why didn't I try it?

Now, with the pieces in hand, it is important to put them into some kind of context. Here are the life stories, or part of the life stories, of six individuals—Bernice Wheeler, Sophia Bielli, Marjorie Pierce, John Lamberton, George Daniels and Dorothy Rogers. The research was carried out over a series of interviews, sometimes lasting a number of years. In most cases the life story has been used to highlight some aspect of the individual's life and to bring understanding to it.

Recollections of a lifetime—those events and meaningful occurrences inextricably linked with emotion and associations that linger—are subtly formed, reshaped and constructed throughout the years. They are not reproduced as a photograph from a negative, but rather designed and painted by a host of circumstances—physical, emotional, personal and social. Memory is at once an introspective and a social process. An event may be earthshattering to an individual. Right after it happens the person may talk it through with others who were there, or hear different reactions from those who witnessed it—all of which may subtly play a role in shaping the lasting memory of the event. Perhaps the memory is that of an uncomfortable, embarrassing situation for the individual, something that with time becomes more uncomfortable, more untenable, a wound that festers quietly in isolation, and something that a person might not choose to discuss openly. Or perhaps with the telling of the story a person's role takes on greater proportions than actually was the case. The individual might become more of a hero, more of a victim, adding the element of a person's self image and reflecting how that person would like to be perceived. Some memories are a single image, arrested in time and remain indelibly etched on the mind, a frozen moment in bright iridescent colors as the scene was viewed by the one who holds the memory. Thus there are many indirect influences that come into play during the final casting of a memory.

A person not only consciously or unconsciously shapes his/her memories, but also these frequently become treasured heirlooms to be shared with a larger audience. As heirlooms they take on a kind of physical shape that once formed seldom changes. A good analogy is that of a large landscape painting. Once the artist finishes the landscape the creative process is done and the painting remains the same. Critics can discuss it detail by detail. Likewise once a memory takes its final shape it is usually described consistently—sometimes word for word in the same way over long periods of time. Perhaps a part of the story is left untold, just as a description of the landscape might focus on a specific part of the painting. Those memories related most often serve as signposts punctuating an individual's life. They are the events of highlighted intensity that the individual wants to expose openly as significant happenings along the life chain: the death of Grammy Wheeler's mother, the burning of the family homestead, John Lamberton's brush with the saw blade while sawing slabs, the death of Dorothy Rogers' eldest daughter.

Along with signpost events come clusters of tales about a particular subject, with each person sometimes only recounting selected parts of the total memory constellation. John Lamberton highlighted a cycle of tales about the lumber camp on Walden Mountain; George Daniels reminisced about Little Michigan, a lumber camp in Pittsfield, and about his great grandmother Parker, who was mysteriously married five times although no one ever remembers her having a husband.

For each person there are also those more private happenings, that only surface after some uncomfortable digging, but prove to be keystones within a life. So often because of the pain and discomfort such memories hold, they are never shared, and when they remain hidden, understanding and communication between the generations is lost. When Rebecca Morse discovered that her great-great-grandmother, great-grandmother and grandmother were pregnant before they were married and wrote about it in the piece for this volume, her grandmother, Dorothy Rogers, initially felt that Rebecca was condemning her. As Rebecca, her mother and grandmother discussed it, Mrs. Rogers came to understand the importance of seeing the pattern and the significance of breaking it. Another issue here is the perceptions of the era. Today, because of common practice, whether one is pregnant or not before one is married tends to be all but irrelevant. It is inconceivable that such an event would change the future relationship of grandmother and granddaughter in the same way it did for Dorothy. Thus new understanding develops not only between the generations of a family but also enables others to view valuable insights into emotionally laden issues of the past.

Today psychologists believe that memory and life review play an important role in the life cycle during the later years. As one ages it is a natural part of the sequence. But for folklorists it is much more than a process. From among the ranks of the elderly come not only the masters of life experience but also the storytellers, the craftspersons, the artists in the arena of traditional learning. I suspect it is the "folklorist" in all of the interviewers that caused each to chose to interview individuals who were retentive listeners, had developed story telling techniques, respected tradition and the old ways, had to some extent learned by doing, and admired continuity. Sophia Bielli was known as Barre's most celebrated raconteur, Marjorie Pierce remains one of the few people who was a participant in New England's musical ballad and storytelling tradition, and John Lamberton had spent a lifetime in a sawmill learning from the old timers and was a compendium of knowledge. Each of the people represented in this collection had lived long enough to have a flood of memories, and the interviewing process provided them with the opportunity to share their recollections, sort them, and place a value on them.

Likewise, we as interviewers are well aware of the personal nature of this kind of research and realize that in recording a life history our role significantly effects the outcome. Our interests sharpen a particular perspective or perhaps skew certain events.

Jennifer Post was interested in Marjorie Pierce's "musical memory" while someone else might have focused on her role as storekeeper. For this reason the interviewer has explained the reasons and circumstances that lead to each one's particular piece: Why was this person selected to be interviewed? What is the interviewer after? Is it to elicit the individual's life story as was the purpose of Eleanor Ott and Greg Sharrow? Is there some focus as was the case with my interviews with John Lamberton about his mill experiences? Or was there a specific aspect of a life that drew them such as Sophia Bielli's storytelling and Marjorie Pierce's musical traditions and the role of music and song in her family's milieu? Or is it much more personal, as with Rebecca Morse, who is after an intimate family history and understanding riddled with emotion and fraught with intricate relationships where difficult questions will be asked and troubling feelings evoked? No matter what the purpose, as interviewing continues over time the relationship between the participants changes. Boundaries change as well. As time goes on, as rapport grows, different kinds of questions may be asked and more intimate revelations may be made.

In the following pieces, different techniques were used. Most of us were outsiders, "flatlanders" who sought out each individual with a purpose in mind. There are advantages to being an unknown, an outsider. Things must be explained, there is no previous understanding of a situation, the slate is clean. At the same time as outsiders we may miss some of the important questions. We may never know about some of the buried touchstones of memory. In many cases that is irrelevant. I wasn't looking for a personal, psychological life story but rather what it was like being a sawyer in a sawmill, what John Lamberton's thoughts were about it, how he regarded it. I was interested in what he *wanted* to tell me, not in probing the more private parts of his life. For Rebecca Morse it was a different matter. She was an insider, coming with a lifetime of experience as a family member. Her own recollections were shaped and her relationships colored by being a part of the family. No wonder the interviewing was emotionally draining and uncomfortable. Because of the personal nature of the interviewing, not all she learned was appropriate to include—indeed in any written work there are always selective choices made. But the results of her interviewing produced an extraordinarily rich piece—not only in terms of family history and understanding but also in regard to her grandmother's ministry of healing.

Eleanor Ott approached her interviewing from a different perspective. Although she was an outsider, her friend Lucille Cerutti was Grammy Wheeler's daughter, and in many cases her interview was a three-way conversation. Ott felt this enriched the interview process and she believed that Lucille frequently asked questions and brought up associations that evoked important responses from her mother.

Whenever a series of interviews takes place, there is a giving and taking on both parts. While at first the interviewing may be onesided, as time goes on it becomes more and more of a two way conversation. The memories shared are meaningful to both teller and listener and the bond developed between the two will ultimately influence—sometimes imperceptibly, sometimes to a greater extent—the essence of that story. Most of us formed friendships that went well beyond the interview format--indeed that ended only at the Great Terminator.

The era these stories highlight lasts about the span of a generation. All those interviewed were born between 1893 and 1912. Their recollections go back to the Civil War and forward to today, but by and large the life they describe is that of the early decades of this century, when Vermont was a rural patchwork of small subsistence farms and isolated villages. Poor roads and slow transportation were the norm. Few had electricity or a telephone. Self-sufficiency, individualism, tradition and sense of place were commonly emphasized. Time was expendable and certainly not equated with money. As John Lamberton's grandfather said, "Time don't mean anything to me," while George Daniels underscored the problem with today as "Everything's moving too fast."

The federal government was distrusted and anyone who worked for it was tarred by its brush. George Daniels "knew the son-of-a-gun was a government man the minute I see him" and John Lamberton poked fun at the government fellows at the mill quoting the sawyer's comment, "Do you think President Roosevelt's in that bunch out in the back end of the mill?... I wished you'd make sure cause for years I've wanted to shake hands with him." He also commented somewhat ruefully, "Back then a fellow could run his own business." Self rule, local politics and town meeting were all important. Each town, no matter its size, had a representative in the state legislature.

Republican politics was the order of the day. In fact Marjorie Pierce's brother, Glendon, tells the story of the moderator in North Shrewsbury counting the ballots: "Republican, Republican, Republican, Republican, Republican, Democrat." He put that over to one side. "Republican, Republican, Republican, Democrat." "Well," he said, "that S.O.B., he voted twice!"

No one had yet heard of waste management. Recycling was standard practice. Indeed the saying was, "Use it up, wear it out, make it do, or do without." George Daniels commented that "when I was a kid they didn't have any waste," and John Lamberton remarked with characteristic understatement, "Them days they used to fix things," and then ironically, "They take the dumps away from us and then make things to throw away."

Money was scarce and barter played a strong part in the economy. Education and wealth were subtle indicators of class, but sometimes were difficult to detect. It was a workaday world and while a farmer's work was never done, neither was his wife's. A woman's life was difficult with constant chores and always the challenge of making ends meet. Dorothy Rogers paints a picture of a dreary world of washing, house cleaning, raising chickens, digging dandelions and eking out a living for her family. Marjorie Pierce comments on her mother's endless series of chores in the home, on the farm, and in the store, and explains that her mother used to sing or whistle when she worked to pass away the time, to please her young daughters, and, most poignant of all, to keep herself from having to think.

The village was the community center with its church, town hall, common, school, general store and blacksmith shop, while family and community were inextricably tied to place. "If anything happened in the family, if anyone was sick, the neighbors always came," said Grammy Wheeler. Because villages were isolated, and transportation was difficult, it was the neighborhood after the family that was the important social unit. Indeed most communities were a tightly interwoven web of extended families. In most towns there would be kitchen junkets or dances at different farm houses during the winter. Sophia Bielli remembered, the Sunday picnics of the Italian community of Barre's North End. George Daniels reminisced about the church socials, card parties and dances, and he bemoaned the fact that "there's no community anymore."

Within the home, the kitchen was the center of the woman's world. Not only has the work load changed, but so has the preparation of food itself. Both sexes comment on this difference. Grammy Wheeler points out "we didn't count calories back there," while George Daniels, whose taste remained consistent with those of earlier days, still relished his potatoes, salt pork and milk gravy. Making applesauce, hard cider and swizzle; churning butter, cooking cottage cheese from sour milk, butchering, rendering fat, making sausage, smoking pork, canning and berrying; making jams, jellies, pies and ice cream; all were part of a Vermont kitchen. Ethnic groups such as the Italians enriched Vermont foodways with homemade grappa, polenta and a love of wild mushrooms.

Along with food and its preparation came a knowledge of plants and herbs, not only for greens—like cowslips, pig weed and dandelion greens—but also for remedies and cures. Sophia Bielli's mother had herbs for rheumatism and intestinal trouble and camomile tea and ginseng for the stomach, while Grammy Wheeler used onions and honey as a cough syrup and sulphur and molasses as a spring tonic. Doctors were few and far between, and it was necessary to do for one's own.

All those interviewed were deeply rooted in a place—a locale, sometimes even a house: Bernice Wheeler in the South Woodbury-North Montpelier area, Sophia Bielli in Barre's North End, Marjorie Pierce in the West Bridgewater-North Shrewsbury region, John Lamberton in the Cabot-Hardwick-St. Johnsbury vicinity, George Daniels in Royalton, and Dorothy Rogers on Trow Hill in Barre. For both Bernice Wheeler and Dorothy Rogers the house or homestead held particular significance for the family. Not only

13

were there a host of memories associated with it, but it was a symbol of the generations and continuity. As Dorothy Rogers stated, "The house has always been in the family. I hope its always going to be." With this sense of place came a strong identity and a feeling of belonging. Like Dorothy Rogers, most of those interviewed can point to generations of relatives in local graveyards or to personal connections to a tight knit community. Although Sophia Bielli had been born in Massachusetts, Barre was her home and her family was the entire North End Italian community.

Likewise most of those interviewed were interested in local history as well as their own reminiscences. George Daniels fancied himself as a local historian of Royalton as did Sophia Bielli of Barre's Italian community. They had lived much of the local history, and they had strong opinions about it. Further, they placed a high value on that history and had sought it out through talking with the older generations. They could sift their memories to enrich it and give it texture, and with their voices they brought it alive. There is something evocative about a voice, with its rhythm and cadence, its pulse of emotion and its detailing of vivid, first hand scenes. Through their interest in local history those interviewed have placed their own life stories within a larger framework of the generations of a family or the networks of a surrounding community.

Each individual in his or her own voice adds a different perspective to the whole. Yet they complement each other as well, adding a depth and breadth to life in Vermont in the early years of this century. Bernice Wheeler during her girlhood lived in a multigenerational household with her grandparents and different aunts and uncles. With girlish eyes she remembers her chores, her routine, her schooling. Through the farmstead there is the feeling of continuity. During the time of these interviews at 95, Grammy-- with grandchildren, great grandchildren and great great grandchildren--remained the hearthstone for her family. She held it together and raised subsequent generations.

With both Sophia Bielli and Marjorie Pierce we see portions of their lives as a frame for understanding the role of story and music. There is little traditional storytelling today, just as the

Northeast Folklore Volume XXX, 1995 *Vermont Recollections: Sifting Memories Through the Interview Process.* Ed. by Jane Beck

Errata

Text following page 14 should read:

narrative ballad tradition is all but a memory. However, the role and place of tradition in the community was important and what that role was must be understood by later generations in order to get a better grasp of change as well as a fuller comprehension of earlier times. Sophia Bielli with her Old World narratives and dramatic renditions of her tales drew family and community together on her porch. Her storytelling became a focal point of the community and as such encompassed a web of relationships.

Marjorie Pierce's life story—so enmeshed in different family relationships shows how songs were learned, when they were used, and how repertoires were developed. Marjorie's mother enjoyed singing, but her songs served as much as an escape for her as for entertainment for her young family. Through her discussions of how and when songs and stories were used within her family, we see how a tradition is shaped. Songs and stories from many different sources were incorporated into a repertoire. The criteria was simple: if a song or story appealed to a listener, it would be remembered, performed and passed on.

John Lamberton framed his life story in terms of the sawmill and his father and grandfather. He was interested in the history of the sawmill through its men—from the ground up—from the work, how things were done, the sequence of jobs, the techniques employed, the skills, the nuances, the humor and practical jokes; the sawmill as a way of life—its peculiarities and distinct personality. He had spent his lifetime there as an active participant and an astute observer.

George Daniels used his reminiscences of the past to critique contemporary life and the present generation did not fare well in his commentary. He was very much a man of his time, a product of generational learning. He, too, was a keen observer and processed what he saw in terms of his own attitudes and values anchored in the era of the first decades of this century.

Although Rebecca Morse points out the pitfalls of personal involvement in family oral histories, she too has provided a context with which to understand her grandmother's faith healing. Without the understanding of Dorothy Rogers' early life—of its pressures, financial considerations and drudging work—the reader would not be able to comprehend the change that her ministry brought about. As she herself commented, "I feel there isn't a greater ministry done."

Through her visions and belief she gained a peace, happiness and fulfillment that was not a part of her own world. Yet Rebecca points out that her personal rejection of her grandmother's road is indicative of a different life style where the pain, longing and hardship is to all intents and purposes absent. Her piece is not a rejection of her heritage, but instead it provides the underpinnings for understanding it.

Together the life stories contained in this volume integrate common themes and refrains of a period that is no longer part of the modern generation's experience. At the same time the life stories form a backdrop, a context for a vignette that highlights an aspect of that life and puts it into perspective. Behind these stories are other muted voices: those of the interviewers— questioning, channeling, prodding and framing the piece. But the immediacy of the lived experience resonates and it is after all the voices of Grammy Wheeler, Sophia Bielli, Marjorie Pierce, John Lamberton, George Daniels and Dorothy Rogers that speak to us and remain with us.

—Jane C. Beck, September, 1993

The Maine Folklife Center
October 10, 1995

"BACK THERE"
by Eleanor Ott

"Back there," Bernice always says, emphasizing the tangible quality of the past for her. The past existed, occurred, not just in a past time but in a past place, the locus; the point in space.

"Back there" is the gold ring that Bernice hooks the finger of her memory into as she carrousels back into her recollections of her earlier life.

Everyone has a story to tell. Whether or not anyone can be coaxed into telling it is another matter, and often the telling is the chance result of the right alchemy of people, time and place. Bernice Vienna Angell Wheeler thought that perhaps her story was too plain, her life, as she put it, too ordinary, as if any life could avoid the tensions and transitions that create a unique fabric of experiences—the highs and lows, joys and sorrows, births and deaths—that make a life and its living. So in the beginning Bernice and I sat with her daughter Lucille and talked while we all squinted over the jigsaw puzzle lying like an unsorted Scrabble game on the oilcloth covering of the round oak table with the claw feet. We tried to begin at the beginning, but when you are the seventh generation of your family to live in Vermont, where is the beginning? Lucille remembered countless stories that her mother Bernice had told her over the years, stories about what it was like to grow up in Vermont before just about all the conveniences that we consider essential today, including the internal combustion engine and all subsequent conveniences, together with appliances and household necessities that electricity provides today. Bernice likes to point out that her family gave her a microwave oven five years ago for her ninetieth birthday. That was about the same time she borrowed her granddaughter's electronic lap piano synthesizer so she could play her favorite hymns.

My first acquaintance with Bernice, whom today the family all call Grammy, was through her daughter Lucille Cerutti who lives in the next town about five minutes away. Lucille and I became friends while we were both working at Goddard College in Plainfield, Vermont, and our conversations over a period of several years resulted in the "Vermont County Calendar" [1] article which began with the words that are still as true today as they were then: "Most of what I've learned about Vermont living I learned in Lucille Cerutti's kitchen." The only part I would add to that now results from those conversations having been transported but continued in Bernice's kitchen where Lucille and I first dropped in for a visit, tape recorder in hand, in the winter of 1983. Although less frequently, the conversations continue in both kitchens now, and so one hopes does the education of this flatlander from down-country Bucks County, Pennsylvania.

If being a Vermonter is a matter of the heart, then I, like many others of us new-comers, am a passionate Vermonter. The fact is that I am a transplant, and a transplant with very little family history or generational ties. But all through my childhood I spent many happy hours with my grandmother's sister Florence Elsie Carnahan who always lived with us and who had been born in 1879 on the Carnahan family farm about eight miles from the white clapboard house in the center of town where I grew up. Although the land had long ago been sold, and the old farm buildings torn down, Florence, who we always called "Midgie", and I sometimes still went there in the spring to see the purple lilac bushes that continue to thrive by the side of the road. These excursions always brought back memories for Midgie of when she was a girl growing up on this farm. So I grew up hearing first hand about a world and a life that for someone my own age might have been on the moon if I hadn't actually been standing by the same blooming lilac bush I was hearing about.

Midgie had graduated as a nurse from Jefferson Hospital Nursing School in Philadelphia at the turn of the century, and her experiences as a nurse for fifty years made her a realist. What she described to me was a life in which woman's work really never was done, nor, so it seemed to me, were children's chores. When I turned to Bernice to discover what I could about her life on a homestead in Vermont a decade and a half after the life on the Pennsylvania farm I already knew about, I wasn't looking for memories seen through rose-tinted glasses. Nor were Bernice's anecdotes nostalgic memories of golden childhood years. Of

16

course we have talked with each other, Bernice and I, about our lives beyond our childhoods, but for the space of this essay I am confining my presentation of this material mainly to the first fifteen years of Bernice's life, between 1895 and 1910, when Bernice boarded out with a family eight miles away in Hardwick in order to go to high school. Eight miles was too far for a daily commute with a horse, particularly when the horse was needed at home during the day. Much about Bernice's life changed from this time onwards, and that is mostly another story.

At age ninety-five, Bernice lives with her two blue and green love birds in the sunny middle room of the old white farmhouse in North Montpelier where she came after she and Raymond Wheeler were married. The life in this room is the center of Bernice's life at the present time. The room is kitchen, dining room, sitting and visiting room all knitted together. Just off of this room is a bedroom and also a bathroom, a neat, close comfortable nest within the larger old farmhouse with its formal front parlor and parlor bedroom, upstairs room full of family picture albums, summer kitchen, and joined-on barn. In the beginning, Bernice and Raymond lived up on the Angell family farm in South Woodbury, about ten miles away. Bernice's father William first lived in the South Woodbury house when he was three years old and his parents bought that house to have more room for their expanding family, moving there from the next farm down the road where Will's mother Sarah had been born. Then when Will was a young man he brought to this family home his lovely new wife Vienna with the long light brown hair. Here they lived with their two children, Bernice and her younger brother Guy, Will's parents (now the grandparents) and Will's brother and his wife and two daughters. There were ten people tight together in this small farmhouse set in its fields and pastures, sugar woods, acres of fire wood and ponds. There was a big hay and animal barn across the dirt road. Especially fascinating was the backhouse at the end of the main house's wrap-around porch.Lucille remembered it well:

> This outhouse was a fascinating place. You went out on the
> porch and out to the upper end of the house, and here was this building,
> like a hallway, set out all by itself. You went into it like an alcove, and

there were outhouses on both sides. The stalls were all pasted with old posters. You'd go into this hallway and see these neat old posters, and then you went in; and there were graduated holes, two on each side, and there were more posters. It was the neatest place!

But Bernice, whose perspective comes from using the backhouse in all seasons around the calendar replies that:

It was wonderful in the summertime but not in the winter. And there were geese at the other end of the shed where you went out there. The outhouse was on one side and the geese house was on the other. The geese watched you coming, especially the gander. He could be vicious.

Bernice Angell, Will Angell (father), Guy Angell (brother), 1905.

FIRST CONVERSATIONS

In the first conversation that Lucille and Bernice and I had together after we decided to sit down and get serious about making some kind of thorough record of Bernice's life, we talked about diapers and sanitary napkins. I was often told by the older women in my own family that something women always did was to keep a good supply of old cloths on hand. Worn out sheets and towels were cut into strips and squares, and the buttons and zippers were carefully taken off of clothes too old to pass on so the material, the cotton—especially the cotton—could be piled away on the top shelf in the linen closet at the top of the back stairs in the never diminished accumulation of old cloths. In my time no one needed these cloths except perhaps for dusting, but before the days of paper towels such cotton cloths wiped up messes, cleaned up after children or old people who were sick, and certainly were necessary as diapers and women's towels. Since Bernice was only two years older than her brother, she would not have helped care for him as a baby. But when she around twelve, she went down to East Montpelier, a good half day's journey with the horse and wagon, to "help out" a cousin who had just had a baby. In those days you didn't go to the store and buy diapers because there were no diapers in the stores, and even if there had been, most people could not have afforded to buy them anyway. As Lucille commented, "They must have been awful bulky. Think of what it must have been like to keep them clean. I mean, that's what you'd use for sanitary napkins too. And you washed them." As Bernice remembered it:

> Just thinking about it, it wasn't any fun. And the diapers, you know, you'd wash those so often, you didn't even have the kind of soap we have today. Diapers were cloth, they made them out of cotton, muslin, they had unbleached cotton back there, that was much stronger there, the unbleached cotton was very heavy. We didn't even have flush toilets until I was married and we came down here to live. Sanitary napkins were the same. You soaked them and washed them and used them again and again.

After some months of three-way conversation, Lucille went back to work and Bernice and I talked with each other and with the neighbors and relatives who happened to drop by, over the next couple of years. One day Bernice sent me to the dusty cluttered bedroom upstairs (now used for storage rather then sleeping) to bring down a thick album of family snapshots put together by her daughter Docie. In one photo (since lost) a ten-year-old Bernice and an eight-year-old Guy stood at the edge of some trees, perhaps the orchard, in flecked sunlight. A wide-brimmed straw hat partly shadowed Guy's dreamy smile. In his right hand he held the reins of Clover, their pet horse A narrow band of sunshine fell over Guy's shoulder. Clover's mane was so pale as to appear tow-blond in the summer light. Bernice at this age was much taller than Guy who hadn't yet started his upward climb. Her long pigtails hung down in front of her shoulders reaching her waist. She had, it appears, her mother's light brown hair, although the faded black and white photo doesn't give much contrast or a clear reading. While Guy gazed somewhere into the distance, Bernice looked out directly with a quizzical smile. She held a small wooden tub, probably full of raspberries. She was reaching down to touch her

The Angell Family at their farm in South Woodbury. Bernice is sitting on her grandmother's knee in front row right.

present, that the real event was happening, had happened somewhere else, and that one was excluded from it. "I alone, in my memories of another century," reminisces Bachelard, "can open the deep cupboard that still retains for me alone that unique odor, the odor of raisins drying on a wicker tray."[2] It may seem self evident to say that in order to have that memory, one must first have the experience itself, of opening the door, of soaking in the pungent sweetness. Hearing someone else talk about doing this, or seeing a picture in a book or on television of raisins drying does not produce the same kind of memory, if indeed it produces any memory at all. Bernice reached her hand into the dark tunnel of the past and drew out "this long box, I don't know what you'd call it, made out of wicker, that hung over the stove where we dried the apples. The bottom was woven like a basket made with holes between the slats, and we dried apples for the winter there." And with this memory for Bernice, there floods a whole cluster of related remembrances, of turning the handle on the apple peeling and coring machine that clamped onto the kitchen table, of the special taste of dried apple pies which some like better than any other pie. Not so Lucille, who had them often enough herself from her mother Bernice's hand, and who hoped never to have to eat another one again:

> Oh yes, we had hard cider, we made cider always in the fall. They used to put raisins into it to keep it from souring. Then we could have it to drink. And then we would make vinegar, cider vinegar, so of course you don't drink that. There was always a vinegar barrel. They put in what they called "mother"[3] and that meant it had to be warm, it shouldn't freeze. It was kept just above the stove, in the room just above the stove, in that room that had the bag of hair in it. Cayenne pepper and cider was what we used for a chill. My father used to give that to us for cold, heat up the cider, it would be warm, with the pepper in it, that was hot.

Memory, in fact, is a strange thing. "Memories are motionless," says Bachelard, "and the more securely they are fixed in space, the sounder they are."[4] The centrality of a house in a family's life is intensified by that family's shared experiences of birth and death.

Work was the ever present reality in times of joy and in times of sorrow alike. In this respect, the centrality of the house extended to include the barn with its animals and fodder. Taking care of the nourishment of ten people and their sustaining animals and poultry—horses, cows, pigs, chickens, turkeys, geese—provided continuity and stability, however much hard work it entailed. The houses, the shelters of each generation contain their own unique mix of food and clothing. The homestead in Vermont of a century ago held many fewer clothes and much more food than such a house does today, and this is confirmed by the lack of closets in most old farmhouses. Even today in Vermont, according to Barbara Carpenter, a farmer from Cabot, we still "spend half the year getting ready for winter, and half the year living through it." The family could afford to raise its food but it could not have afforded to buy it. Thus, obtaining and preserving food was the full time business of the family; it bought little that it did not produce itself, and it bought that little from a few cash crops set aside for the purpose. Once in a great while a cash crop brought in a totally unanticipated return:

> **Bernice**: We learned to harness the horse when we had to stand on a box to put the bridle on. My younger brother, Guy and I, it was our duty, when we were still quite young, to harness the horses and take the cream down to the creamery. We didn't have a separator then. My aunt had to hand skim the cream off the milk. After the cream had been taken off, it was our duty to take it. This was part of our income, the family's income. We felt that we were helping, and that was the idea behind it. We knew it even then. It wasn't pretend help, it was real help.
>
> Another task that my brother and I had to do was in the summer, and on Saturday during the school year. The family—we used to raise our corn, wheat, and oats also. When we were old enough, my brother and I would take the corn and wheat down to East Calais and have it ground with the mill stone. You go in there now, they still have that stone there. We called it the grist, it went to the grist mill. The oats were used for the horses. We used the corn and the wheat ourselves.
>
> In the summertime also we had to watch the turkeys because they would stray away to the neighbors. We raised the turkeys to dress them and send them to market in Boston. Part of our family's income was to raise these turkeys and send them to market, especially for Thanksgiving. On a holiday, that was always a big day, we would usually have chicken. Occasionally we probably ate a turkey, once in a while we would eat a goose, but the turkeys we sent to Boston, that was one of our incomes. When we sent these turkeys to Boston to be sold, inside of one of the turkeys I put a little letter and my address. I wrote a little letter and said my brother and I'd watched the turkeys and taken care of them. I was quite young then, so they all helped me do it. It was quite interesting and it was quite a thrill. Because a lady in Boston that bought our turkeys answered me. This lady sent me back a beautiful doll, a china one, just about eight inches long. She had beautiful clothes, dresses that were lovely and a velvet coat and velvet hat. She wrote me a letter back and sent me this doll.

Bernice and I both brought to these conversations an appreciative interest in how people managed in the past to cope with the vicissitudes of Vermont winter and the unpredictable, unreliable nature of the rest of the seasonal round. Our

perspectives were of course different, shaped by a different time
and by different places. In Vermont, the fickleness of seasons is
considerable. Bernice had her own way of doing things tested
down the generations and defined by her own lifetime of
experience. I wanted to understand both the how and why of what
she did. Mine was not objective research, nor even curiosity, but
survival. I figured that talking with someone who had come
through ninety-odd years of living could pass on this knowledge.
Bernice never let me down:

THE CELLAR

We used to spend a lot of time getting things ready for down
cellar. We used to have a big bin of potatoes and a big crock with salt
pork. And apples were on the shelves. There were Pound Sweets, and
Russetts, and Astrachans.

The potatoes were just put loose in the bin. We didn't used to put
carrots in sand or sawdust back there because our cellar was much
cooler, you see, there wasn't any heat. We put stuff up in jars, some, but
not as much as we do now. That would be about all that we could throw
down in the cellar. Squash would go upstairs somewhere. They never
put squash in the cellar, squash got to be in a dry place. Then we
butchered the beef, and the pork, and we would wrap the meat in the
newspaper, and freeze it, and put it in an oat bin when we had fresh
binned oats. We would put it in there after it was frozen. This would
be in December when it would freeze hard. Wrapped in newspaper and
buried in the oats.

We raised pigs and we butchered what we needed for food in the
fall. The sow, and any others, we kept them all winter because we'd
keep them down in the horse manure. There's always a lot of heat in
horse manure, and that would be down in the basement of the barn. The
little pigs wouldn't come until spring. We did the butchering right there
ourselves. The hams we would make up into pickle and into bacon.
Then of course there was the salt pork we'd put down in the crock. Then
the pieces of meat that we would cook, pieces of fresh pork not put in
the brine and smoked, we would preserve. We'd wrap it all in
newspaper and freeze it hard and put it up in the oat bin in the barn. We
really wouldn't slaughter them until it was cold enough to freeze them,
very cold. The hams never went into the oat bin, we never froze those.
They would be put into this brine, salt and sugar and saltpeter. Salt
pork is put down in just salt, water and salt.

You have to be careful not to leave the ham in too long because
the ham would harden. We just didn't ever leave it too long. You had
to be careful or it could be too salty, or too tough. There's a real art and

trick to using that brine. You only knew by practice and leaving it in so many weeks. We'd keep track of how many weeks the ham had been in and we knew it would be okay. Then we took it out of the brine and smoked it. Back there when we raised the pigs, we kept them until they were larger, so our hams would be a pretty good size. So it was another few weeks that we smoked them.

Bernice and I would often get together with her daughter Lucille in the evening, or on Saturdays, so that we could re-visit that early world with Lucille, who had heard so many of these stories when she herself was a child. We all enjoyed this strategy, and our three-way conversations produced a multi-textured picture. One of the reasons this strategy worked was that Bernice continued to carry on, to practice many of the cooking and living habits that she had learned as a child growing up on the homestead. Thus, not all that we talked about was in the past; much of it was also in the present. Bernice was married right after the First World War, but she didn't live in a house with electricity until almost ten years later. Another reason this strategy worked was that Lucille clearly remembered going to the South Woodbury farmhouse when she was a child, so that her images of the details of the farm come from her own experience and not just from her mother's telling about it. A third reason is that after her marriage Lucille continued to live in much of what we might term this older country way. Putting food by for the winter, for example, seemed like common sense, was frugal, was dictated by necessity, and produced the kind of food Lucille wanted her family to eat. Some of the things that were salvaged from the homestead are in Bernice's house and barn, and some are in Lucille's. These artifacts are tangible reminders of that place and time:

> **Lucille:** There's a barrel up in the top of our barn now; when you take the cover off, it smells just like it's been used for smoking stuff. I remember we always used to put the hams and the bacon down in the brine and then smoke them. We were upstairs the other day in our barn looking around and we took this old canvas off this barrel. The old oak smelled just like it did when I was young. Of course we used to smoke with corn cobs. You raised corn and saved the cobs and smoked your stuff with corn cobs. You'd take a metal plate and put it in the barrel. You'd go into the house and get the ashes, get some hot coals out of the stove, and just have a smoldering little fire with your corn cobs, right

inside the wooden barrel, the one up there in the barn. Well, the trick is the brine. (*Reading from the little green card file of recipes:*)

Pickle for Ham:

100 lbs. meat
8 lbs. salt
1 qt. molasses
4 gal. water
5 oz. saltpeter

Bernice: That would have been packing salt. Usually a country store would have that, and saltpeter.

Lucille: It's canning salt. It hasn't got so much stuff in it, it's not iodized, and pulverized. Basically that's what we do when we put salt pork down. We go to the feed store and buy packing salt, cause it takes a lot of it, you buy twenty-five pounds of packing salt. Let boil and skim. You probably did that to melt the salt and the molasses and the saltpeter before you put it in the meat.

Bernice: You let it cool first before you put the meat in it. Probably you might have had to turn the meat from time to time, but the brine would be enough to cover it, completely. About six weeks it sat in the brine, and then we smoked it.

Lucille: See that's another thing they don't ever talk about in any of these books, is those old cellars were cool. And they were a great place. Like the potato bin, you didn't have to think about sprouting potatoes till late spring because it was so nice and cool down there.

Bernice: The potatoes were just open there in the bin. We had a big bin, we didn't put any covering of any kind over them.

Lucille: There was a crock down cellar that had pickles in it, from cucumbers. People had a line of crocks down cellar. There'd be one with salt pork, and there'd be one with pickles.

Bernice: We hadn't taken the burp out of the cucumber yet. Upstairs in winter was like a refrigerator. So much of our upstairs rooms, like this back room I've told you about where we used to keep things in summer, it would freeze in winter. In winter we'd keep those things down cellar. The butter would go down cellar, we didn't want that to freeze. And milk and cream would all go down cellar in winter.

Lucille: There were things on the cellar stairs. The cellar had the old stone foundation and dirt floor. They banked every house before the winter, usually with hay, to keep it from freezing.

Bernice: And there used to be one thing that would stand in the bottom of the stairs for winter use, a pail of lye soap. I used to help my grandmother make this lye soap. Outside we had this little lye house made of wood with a metal sieve toward the bottom. We would dump the ashes in there and we would pour water into the ashes and the lye from the ashes would leach into the water and run out the bottom. Then she would boil this lye water in a big kettle outside and she would mix it with tallow when we butchered. It was awfully strong. It would eat the hide right off you. I have to tell you what good old Clover our horse did. You know, we put the lye in a barrel. Clover was very inquisitive for a horse, so that she found herself the barrel and stuck her tongue in the lye. That was a terrible day, poor thing. You couldn't do anything for her. It healed, but she ran round and round and round. She was in agony, of course she was.

KITCHEN

Upstairs from the cellar, but not over the cellar, was the kitchen where much of the preparation of the food that went into the cellar crocks took place. The kitchen was the center of the house, what Bachelard calls "a center of magnetic force...a major zone of protection." It was the house's main alchemical chamber, for here, daily, substances of one composition were changed into substances of another composition. Every day the milk of fourteen cows came in. Actually, the family sold the greatest volume of that milk and cream:

> **Bernice:** My father would have this can of milk that we would start out with in the morning. Up in Woodbury Center at one time when the quarries were running, there were a lot of people up in there. He would go to the houses and they would come out with their dish and he would measure out of this can whatever they wanted and dip it out, a quart, or a pint. My father had a measure and he would dip out of this can. I used to go with him quite often to deliver the milk to Woodbury Center. He delivered to probably twenty-five people. I can't seem to remember if we went in the winter, but I imagine he did. These were just local families that didn't have their own cow, that worked on the quarries.

Milk they sold on the milk route, and cream they sold to the creamery. The rest of the milk and cream each day the women and children in the kitchen had to transform into some other form that would keep longer and that was not as perishable as the liquid milk in its unending flow. Bernice and Lucille talked with each other about some of these strategies for the conversion of milk:

> **Bernice:** We didn't make hard cheese, we'd make what we called cottage cheese. That was like any cottage cheese that you buy, only we

26

made it from sour milk. We soured the milk and made it from that.
We'd just let the milk set until it would get sour, in a warm place, and
then it was heated to a certain degree.

Lucille: Set there on the back side of the stove, on the wood stove,
back by the water reservoir. Then it would get kind of lumpy and you'd
put it through the cheese cloth. Then they'd put cream back into it. Not
that it's hard to make, but you got to have raw milk. See it was set way
back, and the stove wasn't going that hot all the time, not way back
there. Boy, those old stoves were something else again.

Bernice: We learned to do everything with them.

Lucille: The reservoir is a tank over on one side of the stove with
a door that picks up. It would hold probably four gallons of water. The
heat from the stove went into the oven and it went over to the reservoir.
That bucket with the sour milk in it used to sit way over there beyond,
over beside the reservoir. You just poured water into the reservoir as
you needed to and dipped it out with a dipper. And lugged it over to the
sink to wash your dishes.

Bernice: Can you tell how hot the oven is from putting your hand
in? That's the way we tested it. If it was real hot when we put our hand
in, then it was okay for whatever we wanted to bake hot. If it wasn't too
warm, your hand would be just a little warm. If we needed it hotter,
we'd have to put more wood in.

Lucille: But how did you know when it was time to take it off and
put it through the cheese cloth?

Bernice: You stirred it up, the curds didn't want to get tough.
They'd be very small curds, very thin. The curds would form, they'd
separate from the liquid. That's why you had to watch it so carefully,
because a little bit too much heat would make them tough. You'd have
to taste it. A couple of hours probably.

Lucille: Now the milk had soured before you put it on there. Then
it formed the curds. You've heard of curds and whey, the curds would
separate from the whey. You'd feed that to the pigs. With the swill
bucket, it went to feed the pigs.

Bernice: Yes, we had a swill bucket in the kitchen, we saved
everything like that. You'd put it through the cheese cloth and that
would take the whey out and you'd just have the curds. Then we would
add the salt, the seasoning, the cream. That's all there was to it. Salt
and cream.

Lucille: And then some of the sour milk that you couldn't manage,
you used to feed the hens. Now if you want to watch something funny,
you want to watch hens eat sour milk. It's the funniest performance you
ever saw. We used to take the sour milk out there to the hens out there
in the barn just to stay there and watch them perform (*makes a funny
noise of hens drinking milk*), to eat that sour milk. It would form the

curd, oh they loved it. Then with all the cream, Ma made sour cream pie.

Bernice: It's made with just the sugar and spice, eggs. I might have it in some of my grandma's cook books. Probably I have.

Sour Cream Pie

1 cup sour cream

1 scant cup of sugar

pinch of salt

1 t. cinnamon

1 cup chopped raisins

1 egg

1/2 t. clove

Bake in 2 crusts

One thing, before we had the separator, we had to put all those pans of milk in these big ten quart pans and set it and skim the cream off. That was quite a job. Then we got the separator, you had to crank that. One of my brother's and my tasks to do at night was to go for the cows. We had a place where we could go to hear the hermit thrush every night, he has a beautiful song. We specially went by this place to hear him sing, cause he quite often sings in the evening. The cows were inside a fence in a sort of pasture. The cows knew it was time to come home too. We'd usually find them in the same place. Sometimes we'd call to them, "Come on, Come on," or something like that. Not many of the cows had names. We had Jerseys mostly, fourteen cows. That was a lot of cows back there.

There was this room called the milk room. There's where we kept the milk on racks in pans before we had a separator. Things were cool in summer out there. In the wintertime that room would freeze. This room didn't open into the kitchen, but there were two doors that you could go through. My brother and I had the task to bring the cream down to North Montpelier to the creamery. There was a creamery for a while in South Woodbury, but there wasn't while we were taking the cream.

Well, we used a lot of cream for cooking. We had a cake that we made so much, and that was to put one egg in the cup and fill it with thin cream, sugar, milk, and saleratus, they used to call baking soda saleratus. It had to be put in water. That's the old name for baking soda, that was the soda same as we have today. This cake, seems as though it was a cup and a half of sugar, a cup and a half of flour. It was very easy to make. We made our butter in one of those old fashioned churns, with the stick you moved up and down. That's tiring after awhile, because sometimes you don't get the butter the right temperature, so it's slow in coming. It would come quickly if you warmed the temperature of the cream, perhaps put it on the reservoir.

Bernice's grandfather and father took their logs over to the Robinson sawmill in Kent's Corner, Calais, to be sawed into boards. c.1900.

The churn was a crock with a wooden cover with a plunger. It made good butter, though, nice fresh butter, from fresh cream. We usually just made it into cakes, about a pound. We didn't have that kind of paper that butter gets wrapped up in. We usually put it in some kind of dish. We didn't count calories back there, we were doing so much exercise.

The ancient polarities of water and fire were the provinces of the women and children. Milk, cream, whey. Solid fat tried out in big iron kettles until it was liquid fat, skimmed, strained, and finally solidified into lard. Apples crushed and cooked down until they became a thick sauce, sweetened, and put away for winter use. Water in all its transmutations was brought in cold from the spring or hand pumped into the sink cold from the well, dipped warm or hot from the stove reservoir for dish washing, or boiled in kettles for clothes washing. Steam thickened the air and presented a constant danger from scalding, while ice from the shed in the barn was brought in to make ice cream. Hot water for the Saturday night bath in the tin tub was placed in front of the stove to prevent the bather from getting a chill. Kettles of water were needed at births, and to care for the sick and the dying.

Whatever food was not boiled in water or fried in liquid fat, was baked in the oven against the firebox of the cook stove.

Bernice remembers only too well the constant vigilance necessary to safely maintain wood stoves in a dry timber house:

Bernice: If the firewood is dry, it's much better. We always got our wood pile out in the winter because that gives it time to be good for the next winter. It needs to dry. That prevents a lot of creosote from forming. We most always knew what to do to keep the chimney clean, so we never had a serious fire. If you keep your chimney clean, it won't happen. They used to take a chain and go up on the roof and get the creosote out, rattle it around inside. Quite often some people used to build up a wood fire and let it burn out, if there wasn't too much creosote there, and you did that often, it would get cleaned out. 'Course we could always be near by with pails of water.

The fire at the farm happened when we rented the place, after I was married and not living there any more. We rented the place, and the people built a fire and went away and it caught from the stove pipe. They were local people, people who should have known better. This was back in 1936. My father, of course, lived there all his life, and he liked to go back there to stay. It wasn't safe for him to stay alone, and we knew these people so we rented them rooms. And he had some rooms there so he could go and stay. He just liked to go up and stay a few days. He was in the house, but there was no one else. If there had been people there, I guess they could have put it out, but he couldn't alone. People came along to help, but it was too late. It was a very old house. We felt very sorry because it had been home for a long time for the family. We hate to see people have fires like that, it's terrible.

When there was a fire, the neighbors all congregated, but they weren't organized; there were no fire trucks or things like that. They would make a bucket brigade and try to save part of the building, but the water would have to come from the spring. If you were near a pond, it was good, but they didn't have the ponds that we have now. Somebody would be pumping the water up from the well and there would be just a line of people.

We had one stove in the middle of the house that had a fire in it all night. Sometimes if it was a very cold night, we would have to get up in the night and put some wood in. The rest of the house was usually cold. The kitchen was closed off at night because it was very cold There was no cellar under the kitchen. It was a very cold room. We let that fire go out at night. In the morning the wash dish would be frozen to the sink. We had stoves in some of the bedrooms, but the big stove, that large stove, would keep things decently warm so we wouldn't be too cold.

My grandmother made these down puffs, every bed had one of those. In the morning when we got up we all went down and dressed beside the stove. Dad would always get up early and start the stove in the kitchen so it would warm up, so it was warm in the kitchen. They would go out and milk the cows before they had their breakfast. So we would have fried potato and johnny cake with coffee and donuts. My father was always very fond of his donuts. We didn't drink coffee as youngsters; we drank milk, or we could have cocoa, but of course the milk from the cow was warm. And for breakfast we would always have oatmeal.

My brother and I used to go out every night when Dad milked. We had this little can, and he would fill it with milk and we would go outside and drink it, the warm milk. In the morning there wouldn't be too much time because we would have too many things to do before we went to school. We didn't usually have eggs in the morning. My grandfather and my grandmother, they owned the hens. That's what their job was, and they had the money from the hens. They usually took care of the hens and gathered the eggs, my father's father and mother.

We walked a mile to school and we had to be there by 9 o'clock, so there wasn't too much time in the morning. Then if we were home in the middle of the day, we probably had salt pork and milk gravy, some kind of vegetable. We often had what we called graham rolls. They'd be like muffins that were baked in muffin pans, iron pans. They were sweetened with maple sugar. They were especially good if a lump of maple sugar didn't get dissolved. We most always had some kind of pie for (noon) dinner, like an apple pie, and we did dry the apples, so this would be a dried apple pie. In the fall we would put apples down cellar. We had these shelves, and apples were spread out on those so they'd keep quite a long while. Then we had the apple sauce and preserves. My grandmother and grandfather had their garden, and they raised strawberries, raspberries, and blackberries. So we had those canned. I can remember as a child, my grandmother used to bring in these big raspberries and put them on her fingers. They were large and they'd just slip right over the ends of her fingers.

When we came home from school, we probably had cookies and milk. Then we'd have supper, some form of potato, and pie again. We ate so much pie back there. Quite often we would have brown bread with it, and my aunt would always make the raised rolls. They also made all of their bread that we had. We had to buy the white flour that the rolls were made of. We had little chores at the barn that we used to have to do when we got home. We used to have doves in the top of the barn; they were white doves, and we had to take care of them. Then we would help our grandfather and grandmother around the henhouse and around their garden. And yes we had to feed the geese. The ganders weren't very sociable, we were always afraid of them. They can be really mean. For playmates my brother and I had a horse and dog.

THE ROOM

Up in Woodbury in the old farm was that room downstairs that was sometimes used as a living room, sometimes as a bedroom. This was Raymond's and my room when we were married and went there to live. I was born in that room; Doris—my first daughter- in-law was born in that room. I was married in that room. They should have left the room so I could die in that room. It's very natural. My Aunt Etta probably was born in that room. My father wasn't born there because they didn't go there until after he was three years old. But Aunt Etta was his younger sister, she was probably born in that same room. And it was in that room that my mother died.

That was very strange, you know. I thought so much about it when Doris was born in that same room. Doris was born in November, snow came early that year. The doctor that I liked was there when she was born. And a midwife, her name was Dailey. She brought a lot of the local children into the world. She'd stay a week if you wanted, if you needed it. Being at home with the comfort of all the things around you that are familiar, it makes you feel so much better. In the hospital there were strangers. Most births may be difficult, but they're normal. Nothing you really need to be in a hospital for. Usually there'd be someone there from the family, the mother, or someone. You really needed something like that. Probably Doris was not born in the same bed. The bed was moved in and out of that place so many times, I kind of lost track of it. It was a thrill to be able to have her there. Of course it brought back a lot of thoughts of my mother and how much it would have pleased her.

If anything happened in a family, if anyone was sick, the neighbors always came. If you had to be up with somebody all night, they would take their turn staying up at night. They would always bring in food; neighbors were more like a big family. Especially when there was a death in the family, there was always so much that the neighbors would do. Some of the women would always come and stay. Very seldom did they take the children to the funeral, so somebody would always take them, until after they were home. I guess that's a good idea if you are there and see it, I guess it's better if they take little children away. But I did see my mother and I'll never forget it.

It's hard to say your feeling because she's there but she isn't, and it's hard to take. I think perhaps you should be a little bit older so that someone could talk with you so that you could understand. I was just four years old. You can't understand why. You can't understand why when you grow older sometimes. We so often ask why. It's just the experience we have to learn.

Death happened to me four times when I was a child. My mother died, and then my grandfather, my grandmother, and my uncle. The others are not so much of a picture as my mother's. But I remember them all. They were all laid out in the home. It's the one way that you know for sure that someone has died, and maybe that's important too. Otherwise you would be wondering. As a child you might wonder where they have gone.

It's strange the things you remember, the pictures are so vivid even after all these years. They took me to school because they knew that she was seriously ill, so I went to school with this cousin that lived with us. They came for me because they found that she wasn't going to live and she wanted to see me before she passed away. I can see this black horse coming into the school yard, and I knew, at that age, that they were coming, what they were coming for. They took me home and took me into the room. It was just a little time before she passed away. She said to me, "Well, Bernice, you'll always be a good girl." That's the last time I remember her speaking to me. She passed away soon after that. Isn't it strange how you remember those things. I was only four years old.

Memory is a strange thing, isn't it? The pictures that you have back in your mind. I remember the bed, and them putting me up on the bed, talking with her. Think of the years ago that was. Some memories just don't fade at all. I can see the team come into the yard just as plain as though it was yesterday. And feel what it felt like. I realized how sick she was. Today she'd have been in a hospital, and I never would have seen her again. I guess the memories are better than that, because I've always had these memories, and these memories have always been good. I can also remember my father sitting beside her in this room after she had passed away and how I tried so hard to comfort him. Sometimes you get to wondering, well, was it better this way. But I guess it is, because you were part of the family, you weren't just set aside, or sent to stay with somebody else.

In talking with Bernice I came to understand that Bernice's intimate relationship with this particular room in the house of her childhood, represents perhaps better than any other image her experience of continuity despite change. As Bernice and I continued to talk together over the months, we often wondered about this difference between the world she knew as a child, and the world around her now—seemingly devoid of or devaluing continuity—that her great-grandchildren and great-great-grandchildren live in. For Bernice, the house "back there" has

perhaps more of an elemental shelter than a house has today, because her house, and the neighboring homesteads in 1900, held within their walls such a high proportion of the items necessary for the family's health, happiness, and survival through the seasons and through the years. Food stored for use from the beginning of harvest one summer to the beginning of harvest the following summer. Medicines and remedies for illnesses, to attend the births and meet the deaths that the coming year would bring, the Bible, the hymnal, the organ, nourishment for the soul; stoves and a year's supply of wood in the attached woodshed, warmth for the long cold season, and for cooking food and heating water; games and books and quiet corners for entertainment and solitude. I am reminded of Rainer Marie Rilke's lines:

> House, patch of meadow, oh evening light
> Suddenly you acquire an almost human face
> You are very near us, embracing and embraced.[5]

The homestead, in all its elemental richness, reminds us again and again by its very nature of the close companionship between its inhabitants, the family, and the natural order, the natural world. The cellar is rooted in the earth and holds within its elements of dirt, stone, and wood the vegetables and fruits harvested of the earth. The central floor of the house is heated by fires from the cook stove and the big chunk wood parlor stove. Here the necessity of fire is balanced by the necessity of water, especially in the kitchen where the family does most of its indoor living and indoor chores. The central floor also contains the room most significant in the house for Bernice, the room which she associated with the births and deaths she had experienced in the house.

Finally when we move up to the top floor—closest to the sky, airy and luminouswe also move back into the oldest memories held in the house, memories contained in the belongings and mementos of her grandmother and grandfather that were once stored in this upper room. From her grandparents Bernice received some of her oldest family memories, stories about their lives, and about the lives of their parents and grandparents. We move now into the little dark closet on the central floor and then upstairs into its crowded closet containing a jumble of mysteries.

THE CLOSETS

Bernice: There were two closets in our house. The closet we were put in if we were naughty was a dark closet, no sign of any window. It was off the hall. It was a very small closet, not under the stairs but beside the stairs. From the front door there was a little hall and in the back of it was this little closet. That's where we went if we didn't behave. That wasn't any fun. After we'd been in there awhile, we'd behave. Clothes were in there. No, it wasn't spooky, but it was dark. Not a very pleasant place to be. My father never punished us. I don't remember that we ever had a spanking. If we didn't behave, we were put in the closet. The door wasn't locked, but we had to stay there until we could come out feeling sorry. A dark closet with the door closed, but it wasn't locked. We had to stay there until we could come out and behave ourselves. You know, we probably had refused to do something that they told us to do. We could come out when we would do it. We weren't scared, we weren't afraid of being in the closet. Of course we knew we were bad when we were in there. And we were thinking about whether we were willing to give up or not. I was in the closet quite often, and my brother was in pretty often. If we refused to do something—some chore that we were supposed to do that we didn't like to do, like cleaning the hen house—that wasn't any fun. Then if we used some swear word, we knew some back there, then we had to stay in that closet. My father never punished us any other way. He never whipped us in the world. When we were ready to behave and do as he wanted us to do, we could come out.

The other closet was upstairs. Uncle Fred had it full of stuff because he was going to make a million some day. I had this uncle that always had a dream of buying something and starting a business or something so that he would have the income. So he would buy whatever it was, and not get rid of them. This was another brother of my father that lived in Hardwick. So he'd bring whatever it was out and put them up in the closet up there in that catch-all room upstairs. Perhaps something like some remedy, or some sort of gloves, some article of clothing that people were using. Sometimes we would get into that closet and rummage around, but we weren't supposed to! There was a trunk way back that my brother and I did so much want to get into, but we never did. And then it burned and we never found out what was in it. This trunk was so heavy and back in there that we couldn't get into it. That was the only reason. My grandmother and grandfather had their room downstairs, but other things of theirs were all stored in this room up over their bedroom, and it was full. There were clothes she'd made. At one time she took the wool from the sheep's back, and she cleaned it, carded it, and she made her sons' clothes. She would make the whole suit, the coats too. Then there might have been a chair or two. Then there was a table that I have now in the living room here, and there were little stands, little pieces of furniture.

THE UPSTAIRS

Lucille: There was a fascinating room upstairs. As kids, before the house burned, we used to go up to a room up there. I remember there was this great big bag sitting over there by the door. We used to make up the wildest stories about that bag. It was full of hair. Yep, your braids, Ma, long enough, this great big wide braid that you could sit on and that was in there, all braided.

Bernice: I don't know why they saved hair.

Lucille: I mean, who knows. That bag was full of human hair. I suppose they probably sold hair at some point. That bag must be after the sale of hair was no good and they couldn't sell it. They'd saved it all these many years. They couldn't throw it away. And there was this shelf that went along in front of the windows.

Bernice: There were two windows at the end of the house.

Lucille: There was a shelf that went there and it was full of all this stuff, had this cast iron bank that was like an old hen. And we, poor old hen, we ran this penny through, we put the penny in and she would [*Lucille makes chicken noises*] lay an egg, right, then you put the egg back, put the penny back. [*Chicken noises again.*] When we went out digging in the dump out where they took all the stuff from the fire, after the farm burned, I kept hoping that bank would show up, but it never did. And the old steamer trunk up there that Ma never looked in. Imagine what must have been in it. I guess we could make up stories about that!

What power and significance a single room can have in our lives and in our memories. Especially in a house where a family has lived for a number of generations, the ambience of a room becomes saturated with the cries of sorrow and of joy that echo there. The great French explorer of the mind, Gaston Bachelard, speaks in a language arising from our common ancestral experience:

> The old house, for those who know how to listen, is a sort of geometry of echoes. The voices of the past do not sound the same in the big room as in the little bed chamber, and calls on the stairs have yet another sound. Among the most difficult memories, well beyond any geometry that can be drawn, we must recapture the quality of the light; then come the sweet smells that linger in the empty room, setting an aerial seal on each room in the house of memory. Still farther it is possible to recover not merely the timbre of the voices, "the inflections

of beloved voices now silent," but also the resonance of each room in the sound house.[6]

Our identity grows out of our perception and memory of our participation in certain time-defined moments in special places. A house, old in generations to a family, is wrapped in an intangible and emotionally charged aura which each member of the family embraces when reminiscing about how life was lived in that old house. Despite the fact that the farmhouse in South Woodbury burned to the ground many years ago, still this house where Bernice once lived embodies Bernice's cherished memories, especially of childhood. The destruction of the house in a sense froze it in time and intensified its importance and value as a place of memory.

When her daughter Lucille and I turned to Bernice to hear her tell us about the times of her life, we always heard her speak about the particular places that impressed her because of the personal significance to her of the events-in-time in those places. "Back there," Bernice always says, emphasizing the tangible quality of the past for her. The past existed, occurred, not just in a past time but in a past place, the locus, the point in space. There is a room in that house that Bernice holds indelibly in her memory.

WINTER

"Winter," wrote Bachelard, "is by far the oldest of the seasons. Not only does it confer age upon our memories, taking us back to a remote past but, on snowy days, the house too is old. It is as though it were living in the past of centuries gone by."[7] This is a sentiment shared by many who live through the northern winters. The winters of my own childhood, even in Pennsylvania, seem to have been cataclysms of wind and snow. Perhaps all children remember winter this way; and perhaps our childhood memory of winter becomes the winter of our dreams and of our reverie. "I can never remember," mused the poet Dylan Thomas, "whether it snowed for six days and six nights when I was twelve or whether it snowed for twelve days and nights when I was six." Exactly!

Bernice: When I remember, the winters used to be different from the ones we've had recently. We used to have more snow than we've

37

had. I was going to show you a picture of what they did to the roads. Of course the men always did a lot of shoveling. In the wintertime the men were opening roads if there was a big storm. But around here the roads were always cleared. I was going to show you how they cleared the roads. That's the big snow roller, and the horses, six horses. They'd go down the road just as we go down with the plow, so it would be set down for the sleighs. So the roads would get higher and higher. If you got outside of where the roller went, you could tip over very easily. That was a lot of fun! The youngsters would like to step into the snow off the road. The snow wouldn't be packed down there. Course you get out on a snowmobile today, you get out in the country. It's nice, it gives us a lift if we can walk out into the woods. We snowshoed. We didn't ski back there, but we had snowshoes. Even as children. Not my father or the others, they wouldn't, they were too busy just feeding us. We all wore fur coats, coon skin mostly, or beaver, mink, otter. When we went in the sleigh, we had one buffalo robe we were sitting on and another one over us. They were quite heavy, but nice and warm. We took with us in the sleigh what we called free stones. They were heavy, soapstones I think they were. They had bails on them, so you could pick them up. We would heat them in the coals and they would stay warm a long time. We used to take them to bed occasionally.

We had three stoves that my brother Guy had to bring wood in for. It was my brother's duty to fill the woodbox, and mine to wash the dishes. One time we did switch. My brother said, 'I think I'd like to do your job for awhile", so of course I was happy to do that, and so we did, but it was just once. By the time Guy got that batch of dishes washed, it was all he wanted to do, his hands were all swelled up, and he wanted to go back to his woodbox. We had a hand pump but it froze up in winter lots of times. I remember the blue agateware pail and the agateware dipper and the old black sink.

Back there, if we didn't look after the fires we knew perfectly well that we'd all be cold. We never thought about getting tired of doing all that. We never thought about it that way. These things have to be done. When we went to bed, we went right to sleep. We were tired, we'd put in a full day.

When I was a very small girl, my uncle that lived with us had appendicitis and the hospital was in Montpelier more than twenty miles away. The only way we could get him to the hospital was to make up a bed on a sleigh. It was in the middle of the winter. The doctor and my aunt went with him on the sleigh, but the appendix burst before they could get him there. He came out of it all right, but he was in the hospital two months. We imagined that was the end, but it wasn't. There was a doctor right up there in the village, but it took so long to go. It took four hours at least. Remember you're going twenty miles.

The hospital was where Heaton House is now. We couldn't call the ambulance like we can today. We didn't have a phone, not then. Not that there was any ambulance.

If you needed some medicine, we had some whiskey somewhere. It lasted a long time. Nobody drank it. Oh yes, whiskey was in the house, but not enough so that you could get tipsy. If you needed it, we had it, if you got a chill... Rhubarb was an old fashioned remedy for a whole lot of things that were the trouble with you. Then there was a powder. I don't know where it came from. We always bought it. It was a brown powder. What it was made of I don't know. I know it tasted awful and that was enough. And the thing that was really good—you, Ceil, could almost start coughing just to have some—was onions, sliced up fine. You put honey on them, put them in the oven and let it cook real slow. It would make a nice juice, and then you let that juice cook out. You put the honey on it and that really made it good. Sometimes we had mustard plaster. We took castor oil. And in the spring we took sulphur and molasses, it was supposed to be very good, supplied some of the vitamins. Castor oil you took all the time, but the sulphur and molasses, it was only in the spring. Epsom salts, that was something we used a lot. You'd put a baking soda paste on anything that itched. But epsom salts were used a lot for soothing. They were very good. And White Cloverine Salve, we used that in so many ways.

In the winter the neighbors would come to visit quite often. The women would bring their patch work and visit for the afternoon. Then of course quite often there would be a quilt to tie. That would be set up and the neighbors would come and help tie the quilt in the kitchen where it would be warm. There'd be four or five, enough to work around the four sides of the table. Then we'd have something to eat. While this was going on, the youngsters, if it was winter, we had different games like crokinole. That's a board game with little pockets. Then we used to play Old Maid and Famous Authors. Checkers, of course, and backgammon we played on the back side of the checker board. There were some jigsaw puzzles, but not like today. We had some puzzles, sometimes we made them, put them on something like pasteboard and then cut them up, but the pieces weren't so small. I had my very precious doll, a china one. She had beautiful clothes, dresses that were lovely and a velvet coat and velvet hat. The doll burned. I wish I had it now. It was a lovely doll. Aside from that I just had ordinary dolls. My uncle had a little wooden cradle that we used to play dolls a lot.

The nearest neighbors just lived down over the hill. We'd get together like all youngsters. We used to meet to go skating. Where you turn to go up to our house there's a little pond. They used to come from South Woodbury, the youngsters, and go skating on the little pond. We kept the snow off that little pond with scrapers. They [*the neighbors*] always used to cut ice up there. Their little house down there was an ice house. They'd store the ice in sawdust. The ice was surprisingly thick; in a mild winter like this probably at least two feet.

SUMMER

After a while we had a refrigerator that had ice in the top, an ice box. We cut another little pond that's just down from below the King Pond, still right down there. That one that's down the back side that you see, we used to keep that ice to go skating. We used the other little pond for ice because it's nearer the house. We stored ours in part of the barn. We built a little area where we could keep sawdust in it. It was like a little wooden shed. We used the ice all summer to make ice cream. My family was great for ice cream. We had the cranking machine. We had to have ice cream. My people were very fond of ice cream, so we made it. Sometimes it took a long time to get it to go solid. We had the cream, and the eggs, and everything, and we made a custard. Then we added the cream and put it into this cylinder. We'd turn the crank and it would be almost frozen. We crushed up the ice and put it all around and then cranked it until it was frozen. We made usually vanilla. We never put berries in with it. I don't remember when I was younger that we ever did do that. We used to put them on the top. And we used maple sugar sometimes.

My folks used to make a certain kind of beer. It was made out of hops and raisins, things like that. I've wondered if there wasn't a little bit of alcohol in it? It went in those old fashioned kind of bottles that had a spring cover. Couldn't have been very high in alcohol. We always drank it, we children always had a little beer too. We made root beer too. We used extract to make that. We made it in a big crock, one of these big earthen crocks. Then we bottled it. Everybody had alcohol, whiskey, in the house for medicine but none of them ever drank it. We drank cider but not after it got hard. We had a vinegar barrel upstairs and the cider was made into vinegar. My father's people weren't as

Will Angell scrubbing laundry on the porch at the South Woodbury homestead. c. 1930

much against things like that as my mother. Her father was the Methodist minister, and they were very much against those things. He preached in Woodbury. He had a lot to do with building that church up to Woodbury Center. Then after my mother passed away, my father spent his life really doing the things he knew she would have wanted done for us youngsters. But his family, probably my grandfather, my father's father, had always made that beer, and so he went on making it.

My father's family weren't Methodists. They belonged to the Congregational Church in South Woodbury. They always worked in the church; his brother was a deacon. They weren't as strict. Beer was always there as long as I can remember. They didn't have it as much in the wintertime; they used it especially in the summer. Over in that camp that burned, over at Sharkey's, these people came from New York every summer. They were very wealthy people. They had servants, they had a Negro servant. He used to have to go to the store down in South Woodbury. He'd walk by, he'd get the groceries and things at the store. He always stopped and asked if he could have a bottle. He wanted a bottle of that beer. He was always given a bottle.

They had their servants and when they used to go by, we always used to be somewhere where we could see they would have on. The ladies, were they dressed up! Of course it was back in the day when they had the horse and buggy. I can see them now with their grand things, big hats with plumes on them and flowers. We had a lot of covered buggies in the village, but theirs wasn't. She had a parasol instead. And gloves. We didn't have too many Negroes around, but they had their servants and they brought them with them. I don't really remember any other families that did that.

THE CONTINUING

Those of us who talk with others about their lives in order to record and understand their form and meaning are only midwives in their creation of their own life histories. We help to give birth to a conscious recollection of a past that might not be pulled into the present otherwise, or that might intrude itself into the present from time to time like a noisy child into a grown-up's conversation, without any intent to notice itself, or to put itself down for the historical record.

Continuity is one aspect of the process that, however long the conversation between the two parties continues, is defined from the beginning, and can only ever be defined, as being partial, selected, incomplete. The other aspect of this process is that I am not only an observer but an active participant in Bernice's universe as it

**Vienna Dean and Will Angell.
Bernice's parents on their wedding
day, Jan. 18, 1893. Hardwick, VT.**

unfolds before me. Obviously the fact that I and not someone else talked with Bernice, and with Lucille her daughter also, made a difference in what we talked about, in what I heard and how I heard it, and in what I choose to write about here. I understand and appreciate this, as I value the friendship extended to me by Bernice and Lucille over many years. Bernice liked to talk about the past, and sometimes in doing so she found a touchstone for evaluating the present:

Another thing, back there we read a lot, and before we were able to read ourselves, our parents would read to us. I think TV has taken away from this for a lot of youngsters. Mother doesn't read to them anymore, not to the same degree anyway. We used to play house a lot. We'd have to have our house, and we'd make mud pies. We'd make little huts, little Indian huts, tepees. We would imagine that these people came to visit us and we were getting this meal ready for them. I do think children do miss something by not using their imaginations. They have to be entertained all the time. It would be better if they weren't. We liked our vacation 'cause we could do things different than when we were in school. I can't ever imagine thinking that I didn't know what to do. So many children come in and sit right in front of the television, and there they are. It's even bad for their eyes, they shouldn't be so near it. We made up little stories. Something the girls did a lot was put on grown-up clothes. They would play they were dressed up to go places. If you could get ahold of some high heeled shoes, and a big fancy hat—the grown-ups were busy, and as long as we didn't get squabbling or something, it was okay. We'd go down into the kitchen where they're working and show them. I think it's a shame if youngsters don't do that, if they miss that. Our time was taken up, we didn't have to wonder what we were going to do. As soon as we got done other chores and things that we had to do, we liked to play these little games...

None of our lives remain the same. Bernice, and people like her who began their life before the technological wonders and horrors of our world were born, have experienced extraordinary changes in virtually every sector of life. If this seems remarkable and incontestably evident to me, it has not escaped Bernice's notice. Although Bernice did not often comment on this factor, she did once, in a way. These are not prophetic words, but they do speak to our common sense of surprise at how the world never stands under our feet:

> **Bernice:** To just think that we used to look up at the moon and see that woman up there. As a child, we never thought that we would be seeing somebody walking up there.

Since this essay was written, Bernice Angell Wheeler died at that age of ninety-six. Her daughter Lucille Cerutti continues to live in Plainfield, Vermont, surrounded by her many children, grandchildren, and great-grandchildren.

NOTES

1. Eleanor Ott. "Vermont Country Calendar" *Natural History*, March, 1981.
2. Gaston Bachelard. *The Poetics of Space.* Boston, Beacon Press, 1969. p. 13.
3. "Mother of Vinegar" is a kind of floating congealed jelly-like cloud that forms in old vinegar. When this "mother" is strained off and added to cider, it encourages the fermentation necessary to produce vinegar.
4. Bachelard. p.9.
5. Rainer Marie Rilke "Letters from the Fourth Year" No. 14 quoted in Bachelard, p.8.
6. Bachelard pp. 60-61.
7. *Ibid.* p. 41.

SOPHIA BIELLI: A VERMONT STORYTELLER[1]
by Dick Sweterlitsch

One morning in June, 1979, I drove to Hope Cemetery to meet for the first time Sophia Bielli, Barre, Vermont's most celebrated raconteur. I had phoned her several days earlier, explaining that I was studying the grassroots history and lore of Barre's Italian community and was interested in interviewing her. She suggested that we meet at the cemetery.

I arrived early, wanting to familiarize myself with what is recognized as one of the artistically important cemeteries in the United States. But moments after I parked my car, Sophia Bielli and her friend and driver Pace Nicolino arrived.

Sophia looked frail as she got out of the car. Standing no more than 5'5", with a slight stoop, she was small framed. A hair net held her gray-white hair tightly in place and, by holding hair from her face, her high forehead was accentuated. Her dark eyes were framed with wire-rimmed glasses that rested on her high cheek-bones. But with an immense smile she reached out her hand to take mine in greeting. With no hesitation or get-acquainted small talk, she said, "Come on" and directed Pace and me to the oldest part of the cemetery.

Shortly, I realized that she was not frail and that she was a marvelous folk historian. For two hours, Sophia belied her eighty-four years by guiding us through decades of a community's history. Various tombstones prompted her to recall bitter years of factional disputes among Barre's socialists, anarchists, and unionists. Occasionally she put aside social history to point out the graves of Barre's finest sculptors. Before artistically notable monuments, she became a critic and teacher, speaking knowledgeably about the various techniques the sculptors and carvers used to produce different effects. The monuments at Hope Cemetery provided a precious key that opened a treasury of anecdotes and significant artistic and cultural insights. Each marker and the names on them served Sophia as a guidepost into the Italian community.

By noon, the tour was completed. The weather had become hot and Sophia suggested we go to her apartment in Barre where she wanted to continue her recollections. Along the way, we stopped at the last mom-and-pop Italian store in town where we bought some Lambrusco to accompany lunch. But even as we drove through the older sections of the community, Sophia pointed out various buildings, such as the Socialist Hall and former boarding houses that stand now as important reminders of Barre's history:

There was a young man—I used to say it in Italian, I'm translating it now—there was a young man who wanted to get married. This lady said, "Well, you can go and get married. But it's going to be kind of hard, I'll tell you. I'm going to give you three oranges, but don't peel those oranges until you get to your destination."

So the man travelled and travelled, and he went across the desert. And he was so thirsty and said, "I'm going to see if I can get some juice." So he peeled the orange. And the minute he peeled it out came a beautiful red-haired girl, all naked. And she said, "Give me something to eat." "I haven't any." "Give me something to drink." "I haven't any." Whisst! She disappears.

So he walks and walks. He said, "Oh boy, I am just dying of thirst. I've just got to have something, some juice." So, all right, he peeled the other orange and a beautiful dark-haired woman came out. She said, "Let me have something to eat." "I haven't any." "Oh, give me something to drink." "I haven't any." So, whisst, she disappeared.

So he continues to walk. "Two of my oranges are gone. I better not try the third one."

So after awhile he spies a big place. "That looks like a restaurant." It is a restaurant. So the minute he gets in there he wants something to drink. So he peels that orange and a beautiful blonde came out. Oh, she's beautiful. And she said, "Let me have something to drink." "Come here, drink, drink, drink." She drank. "Now I want something to eat." Well, he gives her something to eat. It's a restaurant, you know. So finally—she's naked—and he said, "Now, you go up this tree and wait there for me. I'm going downtown and get you some clothes.

Meantime, there's a lady that is working there and she's got a stepdaughter who's very, very homely. And she sees this young girl who went up the tree. So she says, "Come on. I'm going to substitute you for her." So she takes a long pin and puts it in the naked girl's head and the girl turns into a dove. So she puts her daughter up in the tree.

45

When the man returns, he says, "Come on down now, I've got some clothes for you." The girl comes down and he sees that it is the homely girl. "But you're not the girl I am supposed to marry." "Oh, yes, yes. You made a mistake. I am the girl." So what could he do? He dressed her. The stepmother was tickled to pieces.

They planned the wedding and had a big feast. That man was so discouraged because he wanted that beautiful girl. As they are preparing this feast, a little dove comes to the window. The chef is making yellow rice. The little dove keeps chirping and chirping, singing and the chef falls asleep. The risotto burns. They smell the burning rice. "What are you doing? You are supposed to be cooking." "Well, that dove came here and now I fell asleep and everything is burned." "Well, you better start over again." So he starts all over again. And pretty soon that little dove comes to the window again and she chirps, and she chirps, and she chirps. And the chef falls asleep.

Finally the groom-to-be arrives. "That is such a beautiful dove

Sophia Bielli, a Vermont storyteller, at age 85 in 1978. (Photos courtesy of the Archives of Barre History, Aldrich Public Library, Barre, VT).

that I am going to pet her." "Leave her alone! Leaver her alone!" "Oh, no. I won't leave her alone." And he goes over and pets her. He finds the little black-headed pin and pulls it out. And there comes this beautiful girl. "So there's the girl. You are the one that did this." So they started again and had a big feast. They arrested that stepmother and that stepdaughter and the man and the girl lived ever after, happily.

Seconds later, Sophia retold "The Three Oranges" (AT 408)[2] in Italian with a Piedmontese dialect. She followed it with a variant in English of AT 41: "The Wolf Overeats in the Cellar."

Pace's return from her downstairs apartment brought about a pause in the storytelling for a few minutes. The three of us went into Sophia's kitchen where Sophia poured us each a glass of chilled lambrusco.

Sitting around the kitchen table, Pace and Sophia recalled Italian tongue-twisters, nursery rhymes, and lullabies. They told humorous anecdotes about the immigration experiences and difficulties the early Italians had with the language. And riddles they remembered:

> There's a little tool that has an eye.
> And every step it takes it loses a piece of its tail.
> What is it? (a needle)
> On the hill there lives a green round thing.
> And in the green thing there's a white lining.
> And on the white lining, there's a pink lining.
> And on the pink lining, there are a lot of little niggers.
> (watermelon)

And proverbs (Pace commented, "When you were a child, you didn't get slapped. You got a proverb thrown at you."):

> Di mi con chi vai; che ti diro chi ti sei.
> (Tell me who you go with; I'll tell you who you are.)
> Chi non ha testa, gamba.
> (Who has no head, walks.)
> Snobbishness is the mother of ignorance.
> The first chicken that cackles is the one who laid the egg.

Sophia went to her bedroom and returned with a deck of Tarot cards which, she said, her husband and friends used to play

"Taroco." She went through the deck turning each card over and identifying the various tarot figures. I asked her about using them for fortune telling. She admitted that she knew the meanings of some of the cards but that she placed no belief in the cards. One of her friends, however, reads the Tarot, but the rest of Sophia's Italian friends joke about the cards more than believe in them.

It was late afternoon when my first day with Sophia ended. She agreed that I could return again to interview her and to bring video equipment to document a story-telling performance.

During subsequent interviews, I recorded Sophia's family and personal life history, beginning when her father, Severino Rossi, and mother, Louisa Kaufman Rossi, and four children left Bisuschio in the northern Piedmont region of Italy and settled first in Medford, Massachusetts, and later in Braggville. Sophia was born there, March 17, 1893. When she was three, her parents moved to Barre where her father found work in the granite sheds as a letter carver.

By 1896, Barre's emigrant population began to swell geometrically, particularly with northern Italians but also with a large influx of Italians who had initially settled in Maine, New Hampshire, Rhode Island, and Massachusetts. Her neighborhood—Barre's North End—as far back as Sophia could remember was purely Italian.

Sophia's earliest childhood recollections naturally center on her family. She remembered her mother's herb garden:

My mother used to have herbs for rheumatism and intestinal trouble. She was very smart about those things. Camomile tea and ginseng for the stomach. She used to send us out in the woods to get a rubber plant. And if you were bleeding, she'd peel it and put it on the cut and you'd stop bleeding. Mother was a mid-wife. Doctor Rate would call her and she'd help the doctor deliver babies.

But the single aspect of her family history that Sophia recounted with more detail had to do with her father, to whom she was close. She described in brutal detail the conditions in the granite sheds under which her father worked. Particularly poignant were her recollections of the destruction of so many artisans

48

including her father—and later her brother—by the silica in the granite. When inhaled, it lacerated the workers' lungs making them highly susceptible to pneumonia, influenza, and especially the dreaded tuberculosis.

Sophia recalled her father's work in the granite sheds during the winter:

> The sheds had stoves in the middle. They had dirt floors. The wind would blow in every which way. And the poor men, they would get up at six o'clock and go to work at seven. Seven to four. Seven to twelve, and then one to four. And they'd go in the morning and be near the stove and you'd burn in the back and freeze in the front. And they'd take chisels—everything was done by hand. Their hands were frozen. They'd get great big—I remember even my husband had a big callous—on their fingers where they held the tools. And they would come home exhausted. And they'd catch cold and die.

Five years after he started working in the Barre sheds, Severino contracted tubercular silicosis. After several months of suffering, he died at the age of fifty-one and was buried in Hope Cemetery along with hundreds of other carvers and polishers, most of whom had died before the age of thirty-five. Sophia talked about his suffering and his loss affected her deeply.

Sophia began repeating the folktales that she had heard from her mother and sister. The tales drew her closer to her mother and older sister Elizabeth, who was married but lived within walking distance of the Rossis:

> Oh, my mother would tell me stories. And then I would go up to my sister's [Elizabeth] and she would tell me stories. And I would read a lot, you know. Not the Italian ones, but a lot of fairy tales. I used to love fairy tales. Grimm's fairy tales and all of those.

Sophia distinguished between "the Italian stories" and the other ones. The former were stories that she remembered learning from her mother or sister, and the latter she learned from books. At first she entertained her mother, sister and then her ill father with her recitations. But following Severino's death, Sophia started telling her stories outside of her family circle.

During summer evenings on her porch steps Sophia gathered

an audience of eight or ten children to whom she told the stories, always in Italian:

> I always liked them and to have children around me. I like to see the expression on their faces. But I would never tell the gruesome ones. I did not like any killing in it. Nothing like that. They'd all come. My mother said, "You're like a mother hen. You always have a lot of children around you." I love it. She would tell us a lot of stories. I've forgotten quite a few of them, of course. She's been gone since 1935, that's forty-six, forty-five years.

Through her teen years, Sophia continued to tell her stories, and her reputation expanded beyond her immediate neighborhood. During the summer, when the Italians held their Sunday picnics at local parks, Sophia was expected to entertain the children with her stories. Oftentimes, she would tell the stories in Italian until some of the younger children begged her to talk "American." Years later when her own son was a child, neighborhood children came to Sophia's house to hear her stories. "I've told lullabies and ditties," she said. "I've said them here [*in her apartment*] to the children, teachers, and I don't know all who."

During the final years of her life, Sophia, in her eighties, performed her stories publicly at the library and in the Barre elementary schools. The Barre Ethnic Festival, a community effort to celebrate cultural diversity in Barre, featured Sophia as one of its major attractions. Sitting in a lawn chair in front of the Aldrich Public Library, Sophia's Old World tales and dynamic performance style attracted a large audience. Now she told her tales in English, but when close friends prompted her, she enthusiastically slipped into Italian.

Because Sophia received recognition for her storytelling skills and because she was regularly invited to perform for audiences, she developed as a raconteur and kept alive a small repertoire of stories that she learned from her mother and sister. By the time I recorded her, Sophia knew about ten tales, although she admitted that she once knew at least twice that number. When I asked why she remembered some tales and forgot others, she simply shook her head and said she knows best the ones people like to hear the most.

Her audience defined her repertoire. But one of Sophia's favorite tales was a variant of AT 513: "The Helpers":

There was a young man—I'm going to name him Harry. He had heard there was on the hill a tower, a beautiful tower. It was rich looking. He went to his brother-in-law and said, "I'm going up to that tower. I understand there is a beautiful girl up there, and I'm going to marry her." The brother-in-law looked at him and he said, "You shouldn't do that. Don't you know there have been so many people going up there and they have never returned?" "Nevertheless, I'm going to go up." "Well, all right. Here's a ring. You keep this with you. If you should need me, take the ring out, and I shall do what I can to help you."

So Harry goes to another brother-in-law's house. The brother-in-law said to him, "Oh, you shouldn't do it. Don't you know you'd never come back?

"I'll take my chances."

"Here's a feather. You keep it and if you ever need me, you take that feather out and ask me what you want."

Soon, Harry goes to another brother-in-law.

"You know you are making a mistake."

"But she's so beautiful I want to take my chances."

"There's a lot of men that tried, and nobody ever came back. Take this little slipper. If you need me, I'll come and try to help you out." So Harry trudges up the hill....

That's the way it began. At one session, Sophia recounted this tale in English and repeated it in Italian. I also recorded in both languages AT 1450 "Clever Elsie" which she combined with AT 1384: "The Husband

Sophia uses her husband's tarocchi to play games, although she knows the symbolism behind each of the Tarot cards.

Hunts Three Persons as Stupid as his Wife"; AT 408: "The Three Oranges"; and AT 480: "The Kind and the Unkind Girls."

Because Sophia was so animated when she told her tales, her performance was particularly suited to video documentation. However our first attempt with camera and lights—something new to Sophia—initially inhibited her performance, but after a brief rest and a few moments of conversation, she quickly adjusted to the intrusion and once again became an animated performer.

Her shifting facial expressions and her hand gestures particularly expanded her storytelling technique. But it was the latter which were the most remarkable. At one moment her hands contoured the outlines of castles and wells. The next their movement explicitly demonstrated the gentleness with which the witch required the kind and unkind girls to fluff the feathers into the air, and how rudely the unkind girl flung clumps of them all about. With her index finger, she emphasized sharp warnings that the witch gave to the heroine, and, with her hands rising above her head and dropping down gracefully, we saw gold fluttering down on the kind girl, and with her widespread hands striking her arms and breasts we witnessed tar fall and cling to the unkind girl.

While performing her combined version of AT 1450 and AT 1384, she mimicked Mary opening the spigot on the wine cask and allowing the wine to pour on the basement floor as she dreamed of her married life with John. She aped the stupid old man who tried to shove a pig into a tree so it might eat acorns. With her hand open and fingers spread, she showed how the acorns fell through the tines of the pitchfork. She demonstrated how a luckless man tried to put on his pants by jumping into both legs at the same time. Each incident and character in her stories, whether the tales were told in English or Italian, came to life through Sophia's performance.

During the video recording session, Sophia kept eye contact with both her audience and the camera. Her face transfigured from a grimace to a smile, from a stern warning to a laugh, as her heroes and heroines survived their adventures. Often she would throw her head back and look down over her nose as she gave out her warnings or cast doubt on the decisions of a character.

Sophia was particularly adept with rapid-fire dialogue. She used modulations of both tone and pitch with her voice to identify individual characters speaking together in a scene:

There was a man named John and his wife. He was a fisherman and she was a housewife. They lived in a little tiny cottage, on a hillside. But they were near the water. He'd go fishing and sell the fish.

One day, he got quite a few fish. Amongst them was a little gold fish. And the little gold fish said [*spoken in high pitched, pleading voice*], "Ah, John, you don't want me. I'm so tiny."

[*Shifting to a deeper, male sounding voice*] "Why shouldn't I want you. I could sell you. You're pretty."

[*High pitched*] "Oh, John don't. Throw me back and you can have all the wishes you want."

[*Deep voice*] "All right."

So he throws him back, and he goes home to his wife.

Through each scene Sophia varied her voice to reflect different speakers. When she did not do so, she used "he said" or "she said" to distinguish the speaker. But her preferred method was to modify her voice.

At the end of the "The Fisherman and His Wife," Sophia changed the voice of the fish. When the fisherman asks the fish for control of the weather, the fish rejects the request in a strong, commanding voice, emphasizing not only the fish's abhorrence of the request but its unwillingness to allow the wife to sway the forces of nature in order to gratify her own greed. Sophia added to this tale a moral, something she did not include with her other tales:

"So it shows that it's not riches that make people happy, but the little things that count." [*Sophia tosses her head back in glee and claps her hand.*] That's it!

Throughout this recorded performance, Sophia speaks as the wife of the fisherman in a harsh, demanding tone. As she acquires wealth from the fish, her voice becomes more ingenuous and artificially sophisticated.

The three characters in the tale are, then, identified not only by their actions and by what they say, they also are characterized by the speaking voice Sophia assigns to each of them. In the end of the tale, she abruptly changes the fish's voice to reflect its powerful presence.   This alteration heightens a transformation in the narrative as the voice suggests that the wife has indeed gone too far in her requests and now a force greater than her greed denies her control over the weather and eliminates the benefits she has gained thus far.   To this Sophia adds her moralizing ending, emphasizing the failure of the fisherman's wife to accept her natural position in the order of the world.   Technically, using different voices allows the narrative to move more rapidly.   But the narrative becomes increasingly dramatic as characters speak to one another without the narrator's intrusive "he said" or "she said."   The listener is swept into a dramatic performance of the tale, not simply a retelling of it. The final moral brings the tale back into the everyday world.

In terms of performance style and techniques, her anecdotes about the Barre Italian community, her family and childhood experiences stand in marked contrast to her old world tales.   The former are harsh accounts that are best told with no vocal embellishment and with little hand gesturing.   These were true stories, whose reality arises not from the telling but from the immediate truth that underlies them.   Retelling these tales is less a matter of developing narrative skills and more a matter of recalling the past.   Whether in response to monuments in a cemetery, a pair of Tarot cards or questions from in inquiring researcher, Sophia's narratives which depict events of her life are strong and direct. They do not call for a dramatic voice.   She speaks about her father and the sheds sometimes with a tone of pity, sometimes with anger. But the world recreated in these narratives is a matter-of-fact world, the world of her personal history.

Her old stories, however, demand a virtuoso performance that draw upon narrative techniques that she developed during her seventy years of storytelling.   Yet I realized that in Sophia's mind the two types of stories—the personal, family and community anecdotes and the Italian tales she learned from her mother and sister—were essentially linked together.

I now understand why Sophia wanted me to begin at Hope Cemetery.   Markers on its landscape triggered her recollections of the Italian community and ordered them into a grassroots, historical chronology.   After we toured the past at the cemetery, we went to her home, where her family and personal histories functioned as a transition from the grassroots communal history to her artistry as a storyteller. Her Italian stories that she learned from her sister and mother were as much a part of Sophia's sense of community as her historical anecdotes. While her performance styles of the two types of narratives were markedly different, the stories were all part of a unified social and cultural history of Barre's Italian community.

In her living room with some of her handiwork on display, Sophia recounts traditional folktales in both English and a Piedmontese dialect.

On November 20th, 1981, Sophia died at her home in Barre. With her death the richness and immediacy of performance vanished. Yet Sophia in her later years, realizing the centrality of her folk narratives and her reminiscences to the history of Barre's Italian community, left for her community examples of her artistry on audio and video tapes. These now serve as signposts and markers of a community's past and continue to provide a glimpse into times lost and of times "once upon a time."

NOTES

1. I want to thank the Instructional Development Center at the University of Vermont for a summer study grant in 1979 that enabled me to begin my research in Barre. All of my taped interviews with Sophia Bielli are housed in the Folklore and Oral History Archive in Bailey-Howe Library at the University of Vermont. I also want to thank the Vermont Folklife Center for making available to me an interview with Sophia Bielli conducted by Tina Bielenberg in 1978.

2. AT refers to "Aarne Thompson" and the number indicates the folktale type. See Antti Aarne and Stith Thompson. *The Types of the Folktale.* FF Communications No. 184, Helsinki, 1964.

FAMILY SONG TRADITIONS: THE PIERCE-SPAULDING FAMILY
by Jennifer Post

Family and community musical traditions have provided a foundation for musical performance practice in northern New England for generations. In nineteenth and early twentieth century community life musicians moved in a more limited social sphere than they do today and stylistic influences on their music were often restricted to the family or small community. By the mid-twentieth century, cultural and economic changes that influenced New England musicians—the ease of travel, and the increasing presence of radios, phonographs, and televisions in homes—offered a palette of styles from which performers could choose. A greater diversification in repertoire resulted. Yet even before the mid-twentieth century, family and community repertoires were shaped by the experiences of each member, especially by musical practices individuals brought into the family or group: a grandfather who had been in the Civil War; in-laws "from away"; a father or son who worked in the woods and stayed in the lumbercamps during the winters; travelling musicians who brought new music into a community, often from more densely settled areas; a subscription to a magazine with a weekly or monthly column that included songs and poems.

As curator of the Helen Hartness Flanders Ballad Collection at Middlebury College, I am always eager to explore New England musical traditions by talking to relatives of people who were recorded by collectors for the Flanders Collection during the 1930s,1940s, and 1950s.[1] In the early 1980s I heard that Marjorie Pierce lived with her brothers in the family home and ran the country store that was attached to their house in the center of North Shrewsbury. Marjorie, born in 1903, was the second child in a family of five children, two girls and three boys. Their mother, Gertrude Spaulding Pierce, was visited by Flanders in the 1930s and recorded several songs known in her family including: "The Half Hitch," "Fair Charlotte," "The Sailor Boy," "Lord Bateman," "The Lawyer Outwitted," and "The True Story."[2] I finally met

Marjorie Peirce

Marjorie in the fall of 1984 when I called to ask if I might come down to talk with her about her mother's songs. Marjorie Pierce and her family have lived in the Bridgewater-North Shrewsbury region of Vermont since the eighteenth century. Members of her family have worked in the home sphere, farmed, participated in the family business, travelled to war, moved away for education or work and returned. Their present home in North Shrewsbury holds family musical traditions which were affected by all these comings and goings. Marjorie has become the vehicle for her family's musical traditions because of her lifelong interest in music, her devotion to her family, and her great respect for historical tradition.

When I arrived at the Pierce home Marjorie greeted me warmly. I was immediately captivated by her energy and enthusiasm about family and community traditions, as well as by the importance she placed on local history. Her home expressed these values too: the warm open kitchen heated with a wood burning stove, the living room and parlor filled with family heirlooms: furniture, braided rugs, an old Estey organ, and family portraits.

I returned to visit Marjorie several times that winter. We sat in the living room or the kitchen and talked about music. Marjorie presented me with typewritten copies of some of the old songs her family knew, sang family versions of those she remembered, and reminisced about her mother, father, grandparents, uncles, and neighbors, all of whom played a role in shaping her musical memory. When I visited in the spring we moved to the glassed-in porch on the back of the house. Marjorie had filled it with plants as soon as it was warm enough for them to survive outdoors. From the porch we looked onto a neatly kept yard divided by a brook and a charming bridge built by one of her brothers. Equally pleasing were the wooded hilly backdrop, and her flower and vegetable gardens. I think we both enjoyed our hours together; Marjorie especially because she had an opportunity to remember the old times, and to talk about traditions so meaningful to her. I learned about customs of great interest to me.

The significance of family tradition to Marjorie can be seen in her precise and poignant memories of each family member, in her care for the ancestral home, in her treasured heirlooms, and in her sense of responsibility for the family store. Family traditions were also important to Marjorie's mother, with whom Marjorie spent so much time during her early years and from whom she learned many of the songs that she remembers today. She was eager to share memories of her mother's, extended family's, and community's traditions. She described herself as particularly interested in history and genealogy and made a special effort to remember the old songs:

> And then in later years I decided I would forget them and so I wrote them down and tried to recollect the tunes. And sometimes it was difficult to get started. Once I got started it was all right, but I knew at that time that my mother's songs—after Helen Hartness Flanders had been here—I knew that my mother's songs would be forgotten, and so I tried to write down quite a lot of them. [April 16, 1985]

While Marjorie referred to her notes to recall the words to some of the songs, the melodies and the events that framed each performance were embedded in her mind. Our conversations made it clear that she has held onto memories of music in her family; they have stayed with her throughout her life.

My discussions with Marjorie between 1984 and 1990 provided an opportunity for me to hear about some of the rural Vermont musical traditions of the late nineteenth and early twentieth centuries and to see how these traditions fit into her family life. Marjorie's descriptions of musical events in her community show different facets of its musical life and reveal a family with a varied repertoire. What she offers, though, is not just a view of the larger Pierce-Spaulding clan or the Bridgewater or North Shrewsbury community, but how Marjorie Pierce defines for herself what music meant to her. Her immediate and extended family worked hard and played little by her definition; yet Marjorie carries fond memories of the times when music was an important source of entertainment for all generations in her home and community.

Marjorie's mother, Gertrude Spaulding Pierce, was from West Bridgewater, Vermont. Her mother's parents, Joseph Kennedy Spaulding and Sarah Aiken Spaulding, lived in West Bridgewater at the junction of routes 4 and 100 in a large house where they farmed and ran a grocery store. Marjorie's grandfather was the postmaster of West Bridgewater for forty years. Ties to the West Bridgewater family were strong when Marjorie was young. Although the Pierces lived in Shrewsbury, Marjorie and her older sister, Marion, were born at their grandparents' home, where their mother returned to give birth to her first two children. They also visited their mother's family frequently, especially during holiday times. Sometimes her mother drove a one-horse wagon or sleigh over the mountain alone with the children to visit her sisters.

Marjorie's mother was busy all her life with chores in the home, chores connected with the farm, as well as responsibilities in the family store. Marjorie talked repeatedly about her mother's involvement in farm work, washing the sap buckets after sugaring, mopping the hardwood kitchen floor, skimming the milk, making and shaping butter, and washing the dishes. Music played an important role in

Home of Joseph and Sarah Spaulding, West Bridgewater, c. 1900. Joseph and Sarah seated. Grandchildren Hazel Johnson (standing) and Herbert Johnson (sitting).

alleviating the pressures of these all-encompassing responsibilities:

Sarah and Joseph Spaulding, c. 1905

> We had a neighbor, Avis Poore, who lived in the little old-fashioned cottage next door that burned around 1957/58. And she asked my mother once why she sang so much, and my mother said: "Well, when you're singing, you can't think." In another words, my mother had a lot of problems in the way of work and responsibility. She had responsibility for the home. She had five children to bring up and wash and iron for. And in those days, we washed by hand with the old tubs, you know. Bring the tubs into the kitchen, get a big pail and fill the tubs with water, and then the rinsing water, and go through the ringer, put the liquid bluing in the rinse water, and go through all these motions, and then hang the clothes out on the line. And that was almost an all day job if you have five children.[4/16/85]

The kitchen was the central room in the farmhouse for her mother, because it was where most of her household obligations were. And it was primarily in this spatial sphere that Marjorie, her sister Marion, and their mother shared their family musical traditions:

> Well, when I was a small child, probably five-six years old, my mother used to sing, and she also used to whistle while she was doing her work. And she sang songs that she had learned from her father, my grandfather, Joseph Kennedy Spaulding, who had a store in West Bridgewater, Vermont. And he was quite a singer, along with his brother, Hosea Spaulding, who played the fiddle. And they used to get together evenings and sing. And it was said that they could sing until two o'clock in the morning and never repeat a song!
>
> And naturally my mother learned many songs from her father and then when she married and came to this town of Shrewsbury to live, and she started to raise a family. During her work she would sing to pass

away the time while she was doing her dishes or baking or skimming
the milk pans—she had big pans of milk with cream on the top and she
would skim the cream from the milk pans—we made butter in those
days—and all that time she would be whistling or singing. And I had
an older sister, about two years older than I am, and we loved to be
entertained by our mother. And I remember so well, that in our kitchen
we had a big woodbox behind the cookstove, and it was a very nice
woodbox. It was painted sort of a cream color with a red trim and a nice
wooden red top. And quite large. And when my mother was mopping,
my sister and I would get up on top of the woodbox and then we would
plead with our mother, while she was mopping the kitchen floor, to sing
to us. And our favorite song was called "Cabbage and Meat," but of
course she sang lots of other songs that she'd learned from her father.
[Vermont ETV, 1986]

Cabbage and Meat

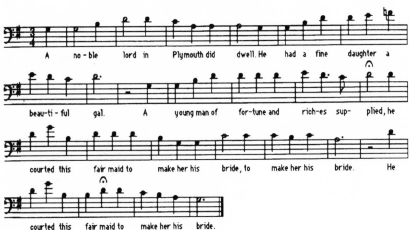

A noble lord in Plymouth did dwell
He had a fine daughter, a beautiful gal.
A young man of fortune, and riches supplied,
He courted this fair maid to make her his bride,
To make her his bride.
He courted this fair maid—to make her his bride.

He courted her long and he gained her love,
At length this fair maiden intend him to prove
From the time that she owned him, she fairly denied,
She told him right off, she'd not be his bride.
She'd not be his bride

She told him right off, she'd not be his bride

Then he said, "Straight home I will steer,"
And many an oath unto her he did swear
He swore he would wed the first woman he'd see
If she was as mean as a beggar could be
As a beggar could be
If she was as mean as a beggar could be

She ordered her servants this man to delay
Her rings and her jewels she soon laid away
She dressed herself in the worst rags she could find
She looked like the devil before and behind
Before and behind
She looked like the devil before and behind.

She clapped her hands on the chimney back
She crocked her face all over so black
Then down the road she flew like a witch
With her petticoats heisted upon the half hitch
Upon the half hitch
With her petticoats heisted upon the half hitch

Soon this young man come riding along
She stumbled before him she scarcely could stand
With her old shoes on her feet all tread off askew
He soon overtook her and said, "Who be you?"
And said, "Who be you?"
He soon overtook her and said, "Who be you?"

(spoken) *"I'm a woman, I s'pose."*

This answer grieved him much to the heart
He wished from his very life he might part
Then he wished that he had been buried
And then he did ask her and if she was married
And if she was married
And then he did ask her and if she was married

(spoken) *"No, I ain't."*

This answer suited him much like the rest
It lay very heavy and hard on his breast
He found by his oath he must make her his bride,

And then he did ask her behind him to ride,
Behind him to ride,
And then he did ask her behind him to ride.

(spoken) *"Your horse'll throw me, I know he will."*

"O no, O no, my horse he will not."
So on behind him a-straddle she got
His heart it did fail him. He dare not go home,
For his parents would say, "I'm surely undone."
"I'm surely undone."
For his parents would say, "I'm surely undone."

So to a neighbor with whom he was great,
The truth of the story he dared to relate.
He said, "Here with my neighbor you may tarry,
And in a few days, with you I will marry,
With you I will marry,
And in a few days, with you I will marry.

(spoken) *"You won't, I know you won't."*

He vowed that he would and straight home he did go.
He acquainted his father and mother also,
Of what had befallen him, how he had sworn.
His parents said to him, "For that don't you mourn."
"For that don't you mourn."
His parents said to him, "For that don't you mourn."

"Don't break your vows but bring home your girl,
We'll fix her up, and she'll do very well."
The day was appointed, they invited the guests,
And then they intended the bride for to dress,
The bride for to dress,
And then they intended the bride for to dress.

(spoken) *"Be married in my old clothes, I s'pose."*

Married they were and sat down to eat.
With her hands she clawed out the cabbage and meat.
The pudding it burned her fingers so bad.
She licked 'em, she wiped 'em along on her rags,
Along on her rags
She licked 'em, she wiped 'em along on her rags.

Hotter than ever, she at it again,
Soon they did laugh 'til their sides were in pain.
Soon they did say, "My jewel, my bride,
Come sit yourself down by your true lover's side,
By your true lover's side,.
Come sit yourself down by your true lover's side."

(spoken) *"Sit in the corner, I s'pose, where I used to."*

Some were glad and very much pleased.
Others were sorry and very much grieved.
They asked them to bed the truth to decide.
And then they invited both bridegroom and bride
Both bridegroom and bride,
And then they invited both bridegroom and bride.

(spoken) *"Give me a light and I'll go alone."*

They gave her a light, what could she want more?
And showed her the way up to the chamber door.

(spoken) *"Husband, when you hear my old shoe go 'klonk'*
then you may come."

Up in the chamber she went klonking about
His parents said to him, "What you think she's about?"
"O mother, O mother, say not one word
Not one bit of comfort to me this world can afford."
This world can afford.
Not one bit of comfort to me this world can afford."

At length they heard her old shoe go klonk.
They gave him a light and bade him go along.
"I choose to go in the dark," he said,
"For I very well know the way to my bed,
The way to my bed."
"For I very well know the way to my bed."

He jumped into bed, his back to his bride.
She rolled and she tumbled from side unto side.
She rolled and she tumbled, the bed it did squeak.
He said unto her, "Why can't you lie still?"
"Why can't you lie still?"

And he said unto her, "Why can't you lie still?"

(spoken) *"I want a light to unpin my clothes."*

He ordered a light her clothes to unpin.
Behold she was dressed in the finest of things.
When he turned over her face to behold,
It was fairer to him than silver or gold,
Than silver or gold,
It was fairer to him than silver or gold.

Up they got and a frolic they had.
Many a heart it was merry and glad.,
They looked like two flowers just springing from bloom
With many fair lasses who wished them much joy,
Who wished them much joy,
With many fair lasses who wished them much joy.

The songs Marjorie learned from her mother resulted from contact with different people in their household, the extended family and the larger community. Thus, the songs she learned have associations with both people and contexts in the family and community. They represent the web of contacts which bind family traditions together and demonstrate the variety of songs that make up an individual's repertoire. Yet there remains an assigned ownership of songs within the family sphere that is demonstrated by Marjorie's association of specific songs with particular people.

> **MP**: This is my grandfather's song.
> **JP**: And did your mother know it too?
> **MP**: Oh yes! Oh yes! I presume that my grandfather knew a lot of songs that she didn't know.
> **JP**: And you spent time with him? You remember him?
> **MP**: Well, we used to go there Christmas or Thanksgiving and then during the summer we'd sometimes go over and stay a week, something like that.
> **JP:** This was in West Bridgewater?
> **MP:** Yes. [pause] But of course, I think I remember him more by pictures. I think I was too young to really remember him. I remember my grandmother, but I *think* I remember him, but I think its because I've seen pictures. I think that's it. This is called "The Sailor Boy."

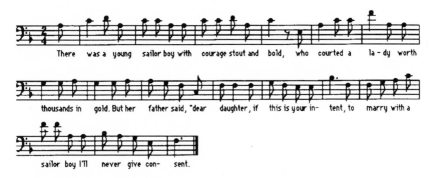

There was a young sailor boy with courage stout and bold,
Who courted a lady worth thousands of gold.
But her father said, "Dear daughter, if this is your intent,
To marry with a sailor boy I'll never give consent."

"Here's twelve thousand pounds unto you I will give
And this shall be your portion so long as you live
My blessing you shall have and your fortune I will make
Provided this young sailor boy you ever will forsake"

She wrote her love a letter though not very long
To just let him know her old father's intent
"But my mind it is sincere and my heart it shall prove true
For there's none in this world I can care for but you."

Said he, "My dearest Polly if you I can't obtain
I'll cross the wide ocean and go unto Spain
And some crafty project that I'm trying out to try
To deceive your old father or else I must die."

He bought him a robe, in spendor did appear
Disguised like a prince, to Morocco did steer
With a star upon his breast went to see his love again
The old man he was well pleased with the young prince of Spain

He said, "Noble prince, if you can agree
To marry with my daughter your bride she shall be."
"With all my whole heart," this young sailor boy did say,
"If she will consent we will married be today."

So then to the church they were hurried with speed

The old man gave up his daughter, his daughter indeed
While the full flowing bowl went so merrily around
The old man paid off his daughter the twelve thousand pounds

This caused the old man for to caper and to prance
To think how his daughter got married to a prince
The old man he did rejoice with exceeding great joy
To think how he cheated that little sailor boy

Then up steps this young sailor boy saying, "Don't you know me
I am the young sailor boy you once turned away
But since I have outwitted you and crafted in your life
I've twelve thousand pounds and a beautiful wife."

"Go to the devil." the old man he did reply,
"You've robbed me of my daughter, my money and my pride
If I had once mistrusted that this had been your plot
Not a farthing of my money would you have ever got.

"Depart from my house and take it long with you
My curses they shall follow you wherever you go
Depart from my house and take it long with you
My curses they shall follow you wherever you go."

JP: So your mother sang it. She sang it like that?
MP: More or less. She had more of a lilt. Some of these were
sung with a lilt, and others were sung very solemnly.

Marjorie's Uncle Hosea—her grandfather Spaulding's
brother—was also an important source for songs and musical
memories in her family. Marjorie discussed her contact with him as
a very young child, but also carried memories of him through her
mother. She referred to him over and over in our conversations:

> **MP:** Another song I remember was sung by my Uncle Hosea
> Spaulding—my great Uncle—my grandfather's brother--who lived in
> the little cottage upon the hill, and as a very small child I went up there
> and he would play the fiddle and sing. The only real song I remember
> hearing him sing was about the frog.

THE FROG SONG

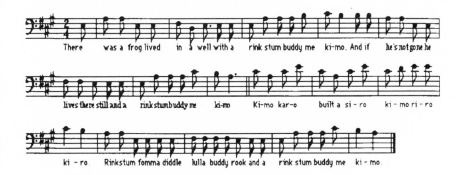

There was a frog lived in a well
And a rink stum buddy me kimo
And if he's not gone he lives there still
And a rink stum buddy me ki-mo

Kimo riro built a siro
Kimo riro kimo
Rinkstum fomma diddle lulla buddy rook
And a rink stum buddy me ki-mo

Said he, "Miss Mouse will you have me?"
And a rink stum buddy me kimo
Said she, "Kind sir, I will agree."
And a rink stum buddy me ki-mo

JP: Was there more to that song?
MP: Oh, I presume. That's what I remember.
JP: And did he sing that faster—
MP: No, he sang it to the fiddle—with the fiddle. And his wife, Aunt Susan, went out and showed us her garden, and I always remember the old fashioned garden with the high, beautiful hollyhocks. She was a little woman, I recall her with her garden, and little old kitchen--old fashioned kitchen.[10/2/84]

Marjorie discussed not only where her mother learned a song and when her mother sang a particular song, but what her mother said to her about the environment in which her grandfather or his brother sang. At one point I asked her what her mother said about

69

the songs before she sang them to her:

MP: Well, she'd tell where she learned them and she told about people who used to come to her father's house and play musical instruments; or how her father used to sing with his brother in the evening. They didn't have much entertainment; they didn't have a radio even, so my grandfather's brother would come and they would sing, I suppose, and while away the time. [10/2/84]

MP: This was sung by [my grandfather] J.K. Spaulding to his daughter Gertrude.... And the name of it is "The True Story:"

THE TRUE STORY

As I went out a hunting, all on a sum-mers day, the trees were all in blossom the flowers were fresh and gay, gay. The flowers were fresh and gay.

As I went out a hunting
All on a summer's day
The trees were all in blossom
The flowers were fresh and gay, gay
The flowers were fresh and gay.

I took my gun upon my back
A hunting I did go
I followed a herd of deer all day
And I tracked them in the snow, snow
And I tracked them in the snow.

I followed them around the hill
And under water went
To kill the fattest one there was
It was my sole intent, tent
It was my sole intent.

When I was under water
Ten thousand feet or more
I fired off my pistols
And like cannons they did roar, roar
And like cannons they did roar.

I fired off my pistols
By chance I did kill one
The rest they stuck their bristles up
And at me they did come, come
And at me they did come.

Their horns were soft as velvet
And long as a ship's mast
Quicker than the lightning
They through my body passed, passed
They through my body passed.

My body was a riddle
That bull frogs might swing through
And when I came to shore again
My naked sword I drew, drew
My naked sword I drew. [10/2/84]

When Marjorie talked about her mother entertaining her while she worked, she was as often referring to a recitation as a song:

My mother also recited poems, Marion and I would sit: "Mother, tell us about the ride of Jenny McNeil."[9-1984]

In addition to "The Ride of Jenny McNeil," her favorite poems included "Johnny Sands," "The Three Little Kittens," "The Two Kittens," and "The Blackberry Girl." In fact, several of the recitations that Marjorie referred to were sung in other parts of Vermont and New Hampshire during the same period. In many New England families there was not always a noticeable difference between occasions during which singing took place and those when poetry was recited:

I was more interested in the words, you know, entranced by stories. I liked to have stories told. We didn't have playthings the way children have today, you know. And toys. Why we had paper dolls and we would feed the chickens. We didn't have all these toys that children have today to amuse us.[10-2-84]

She laughs and laughs when she recalls the lines of some of the ballads like "Billy Grimes the Drover" (which her mother recited) or "Learning McFadden to Waltz" (which she sang). In Marjorie's family, her mother was the storyteller. While our conversation might stray away from her mother's songs to reveal other sources for Marjorie's musical domain, it always seems to return to those songs/stories she most enjoyed:

Well, of course we always wanted our mother to sing the "Cabbage and Meat Song." That was our very, very favorite. But, I liked "Fair Charlotte." I was quite thrilled with poor Charlotte freezing to death. And that was supposed to have happened down near Ludlow, but there are many different places that have been claimed as the scene where Charlotte froze to death. But that was very touching, you know. And we liked those old stories.

FAIR CHARLOTTE

Young Charlotte dwelt on the mountain side
In a lone and dreary spot.
No dwellings there for three miles round
Except her father's cot.

And yet on many a winter's eve
Young swains would gather there
For her father kept a social board,
And Charlotte she was fair.

Her father loved to see her dressed
Fine as a city belle
For she was the only child he had
And he loved his daughter well.

At a village inn fifteen miles off
There's a merry ball tonight.
The air without is freezing cold,
But the hearts are warm and light.

'Twas New Year's Eve, the sun went down

And she sat with a restless eye
As along the frosty window panes
The merry sleighs passed by.

"Why sit there with a restless air?"
When a well-known voice she heard—
Then dashing up to her father's door
Young Charlie's sleigh appeared.

"Now Charlotte dear," her mother said,
"This blanket 'round you fold
For 'tis a fearful night abroad
And you'll take your death a'cold."

"Oh no, oh no, " fair Charlotte said,
And she laughed like a gypsy queen,
"For to ride in garments muffled up
I never will be seen."

"My silken coat is quite enough
'Tis lined you know throughout.
Besides I have a silken shawl
To wrap my face about."

With gloves and bonnet being on,
She jumped into the sleigh
Away they glide o'er the mountain side
And over the hills away.

There is music in the sound of bells.
What a crash the runners make!
The air without is freezing cold
Which caused the sleigh to creak.

With muffled faces silently
Five cold long miles were passed
When Charles, in these few feeble words
Their silence broke at last.

"Such a night as this I never knew—
My reins I scarce can hold."
And Charlotte said in a feeble voice,
"I am exceeding cold."

Then he cracked the whip and urged his steed
Much faster than before
Until another five long miles
In silence they rode o'er.

"How fast," said Charles, "the freezing air
Is gathering on my brow."
And Charlotte said in a feeble voice,
"I'm growing warmer now."

Then o'er the hills in the frosty air
All by the cold starlight
Until at length the village inn
And ballroon were in sight.

They reached the inn and Charles sprang out
And gave his hand to her.
"Why sit she there like a monument
That has no power to stir?"

He called her once, he called her twice,
But she answered not a word.
He called for her hand again and again,
But still she never stirred.

He took her hand in his, O God!
It was as cold as stone.
He tore the mantle from her face
And the pale stars on her shone.

Then quickly to the lighted hall
Her lifeless form he bore.
Fair Charlotte was a frozen corpse
And words spoke never more.

Then he sat himself down by her side
And the bitter tears did flow.
Said he, "My young intended bride
I never more shall know."

Then he put his arm around her waist
And kissed her marble brow,
And his thoughts went back to where she said,
"I'm growing warmer now."

Then he carried her out into the sleigh
And with her he drove home.
And when he reached her father's door,
Oh how her parents mourned.

They mourned the loss of their daughter dear,
And Charles mourned in the gloom
Until at length his heart did break
And they slumbered in one tomb.[3]

We loved **Fair Charlotte** because my grandmother said she knew
a woman who knew a woman who was in the hall when she
[Charlotte] was brought in.[9-84]

Marjorie's father, Willie Pierce, and his family were both long-time Shrewsbury residents. In fact, her paternal grandmother, Demaris Aldrich Pierce, was the great-granddaughter of one of the original settlers of Shrewsbury:

My father was a Shrewsbury man. He lived on a farm his father owned. There was a little cheese factory [Northam Cheese Factory] owned by my great uncle. and my father learned to make cheese there. He then went to a West Bridgewater factory to make cheese. It was in West Bridgewater that he met my mother.[9-84]

After he was married her father and grandfather continued to farm until 1918 when her father bought the North Shrewsbury store. At that time the family moved from the farm to the home that Marjorie now lives in. Willie Pierce was a busy man, although he sometimes relaxed in the evening by singing songs and accompanying himself on his guitar. He also liked to dance and taught Marion and Marjorie to waltz:

Well, my father, he wasn't any musician, but he did have a guitar and he used to play the guitar some. And there were two or three different old tunes that he sang. But they wouldn't be so old as some of these I just told about. The only one I remember was "Daisy."

Daisy, Daisy, give me your answer true
I'm half crazy over the love of you.

It won't be a stylish marriage
I can't afford a carriage
But we'll look neat, upon the seat
Of a bicycle built for two.[10-2-84]

Edwin Pierce and Willie Pierce Farm, North Shrewsbury.

Other memories which she related to me from her father's side of the family, came from her grandfather, Edwin Pierce. Her grandfather's experiences in the Civil War made a strong impact on the family:

Well, my father's father was Edwin Pierce and he was born and brought up in Shrewsbury, Vermont, and he lived in this town and he was a volunteer, and he went to the Civil War and was in the Battle of Gettysburg and Pickett's Charge, which was a terrible, terrible conflict. And he never talked about it too much when he came home, but I know—I learned from my aunt—a few little details about the war. And one was that when he came home from the war he must have come up through Cuttingsville, which is in the village in our town. He must have come home by train, and when he walked from Cuttingsville up to his home in North Shrewsbury, which would be a distance of four miles, and he was actually exhausted by the trip evidently—I know they said that when he reached the house—they didn't know he was coming. When he reached the house he opened the door and fell in flat on his face. He was so exhausted. And of course the family was very surprised and happy to see him return.

And one other little incident I remember is that we used to ask him about the Battle of Gettysburg and he said that there was a fearful battle and that he was crouched behind a stone wall—I think it was near what history books call the Peach Orchard—and the opposing army was marching up in closed ranks and with a cannon, and when they got to a certain distance away they fired. The cannon went off and the air was filled with smoke and the bullets were coming in all directions, and we asked him if he wasn't afraid and if he didn't want to run—and he said yes, he wanted to run, but he was too proud. And when the smoke cleared away he looked down to his friend and companion who was beside him—his name was Billy Cairns—and he had a bullet in his forehead.[12-1-84]

Marjorie has vivid memories of her grandfather singing in the evening when they lived up on the farm. In fact, her slow and gentle renderings of his songs seemed to be the most carefully executed of all those she sang for me. She appeared to be recreating the moment—the song and its context—rather than simply delivering a song from her memory:

I recall up on the farm, going into the apartment where my grandparents lived—we lived on one side of the house and my grandparents had an apartment on the other side—and I remember him sitting in the rocking chair in the evening after work was done, and he would be singing more or less to himself. He sang only two songs that I remember. One was "Tenting Tonight":

Tenting Tonight

Tenting tonight, tenting tonight
Tenting on the old camp ground

Dying tonight, dying tonight
Dying on the old camp ground.

And the other song I remember that was his favorite was Beulah Land:

Beulah Land
I see the land of corn and wine
And all its joys they will be mine
There dawns again one blissful day
When earth's dark cares have passed away.

Oh Beulah land, fair Beulah land

—like that.
JP: He used to rock and sing?
MP: He would rock in the old Massachusetts rocking chair, yes.
JP: Did you sit and listen to him or—
MP: Oh, I would be sitting very quietly and listening, perhaps
behind his back. He didn't hear me, or know I was there. Yes.[1986]

Folk song collectors from the early part of the twentieth
century have created an impression that music in families like
Marjorie's was limited to the "old songs": songs brought by settlers
from the British Isles between the seventeenth and nineteenth
centuries. These songs include the Child ballads like "The Half
Hitch" or "Lord Bateman," and broadside ballads like "The Sailor
Boy" or "The Boston Burglar." More recent interviews with
relatives of singers who were actively singing in families at the turn
of the century reveal a considerably more diverse repertoire. A
variety of musical genres were represented, including locally
created songs, religious songs, and a wide repertoire of American
songs popular between the 1890s and the 1930s. Like many others
in Vermont, the Pierce and Spaulding families did not always
differentiate among these song types, although Marjorie indicated
to me that she became aware of these categories through her
contact with Helen Hartness Flanders:

MP: I have this little song about "Two Little Girls in Blue." It's
not such an old song, but it's a song that my mother used to sing.
Although I think it dates more recently.
JP: When did she sing this song?
MP: Oh, probably 1908-09, along in there—
JP: And again, while she was working?
MP: Oh, always, always. Or when, after—in the evening, when
we had nothing else to amuse ourselves, or it was too cold to go
outdoors, we would beg her to sing.

78

JP: So you would sit around in the living room?

MP: Oh yes. Yes. Do you want to hear the "Two Little Girls in Blue?" I've forgotten the tune of everything except the chorus, and I'm not sure that my mother knew anything but the chorus tune, because I think she recited the verse. As I recall, this is called "Two Little Girls in Blue." A rather sad little item.

TWO LITTLE GIRLS IN BLUE

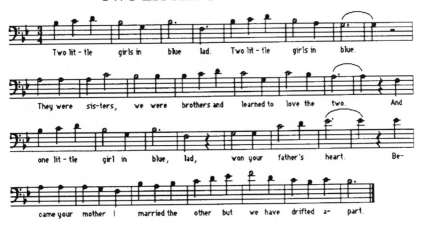

Two lit-tle girls in blue lad. Two lit-tle girls in blue. They were sis-ters, we were brothers and learned to love the two. And one lit-tle girl in blue, lad, won your father's heart. Be-came your mother I married the other but we have drifted a-part.

[spoken]
An old man gazed at a photograph
On a locket he'd worn for years
His nephew asked him the reason why
That picture should cause him tears.
"Come listen," he said, "and I'll tell you lad
A story that's old, but true
Your father and I at a school one day
Met two little girls in blue."

(chorus)
"Two little girls in blue, lad,
Two little girls in blue
They were sisters, we were brothers
And learned to love the two
And one little girl in blue, lad,
Won your father's heart
Became your mother. I married the other
But we have drifted apart."

"That picture was one of those girls," he said

79

"To me she was once a wife
I thought her unfaithful, we quarreled, lad
And parted that night for life.
A fancy of jealousy wronged a heart
A heart that was good and true
For no better girls ever lived than they
Those two little girls in blue."

"Two little girls in blue, lad,
Two little girls in blue
They were sisters, we were brothers
And learned to love the two
And one little girl in blue, lad
Won your father's heart
Became your mother, I married the other
But we have drifted apart." [10-2-84]

Early twentieth century collectors looking exclusively for songs passed orally in families also contributed to an incomplete view of the sources for songs and dance tunes popular during that time. We know today that songs defined as family or community songs were *not* all learned orally, nor did they all come from within a family sphere. The repertoire that each individual took away from an experience in a household or community, even during the nineteenth and early twentieth centuries, resulted not only from experiences with relatives and friends, but also from contact with printed media—such as sheet music, magazines and newspapers with weekly song entries; the radio and the Victrola; as well as travelling musicians.

Marjorie and I talked about songs her family knew that were learned from printed song collections, including hymnbooks and songsters. She mentioned titles such as "The Faded Coat of Blue," "The Rose of Tralee," "They Never Told a Lie," "The Spanish Cavalier," and "The Orphan Children": [4]

JP: What about other songs that you sang?
MP: Ah, let's see now. I can tell you about a song that my mother used to sing, and it's about fishing—some fishermen. And of course she heard that when she was a young girl. This song was sung by a man by the name Azro Maxham, and he was the brother of Uncle Hosea's wife, Susan. He used to be a campaign singer and was doorkeeper at the

House of Representatives in Washington. He sang this song about fishermen once at the North Shrewsbury-Northam church at a concert he was giving. This song is entitled "They Never Told a Lie." And so it goes like this:

THEY NEVER TOLD A LIE

Two wily fishermen they went forth
To the sparkling stream where fish are caught
For they oft told of things they'd done
The times they'd fish and the fish they'd won.
For there never was a fisherman but knew the spot
The times, the place that fish were caught
But they never told a lie,

They never told a lie
They were Sunday school scholars every one
And they followed in the steps of Washington
But they never told a lie.

They fished all day in the red hot sun
The number they caught it was not one
And homeward stopped at a market shop
And out of the icebox they bought a lot
Just to show their friends what they had caught

81

But they never said a word about what they bought
But they never told a lie.

Their friends flocked 'round expectantly
A wonderful mess of fish to see
But as each one gazed they held their nose
Now what was the matter do you suppose
For they didn't smell as sweet as fresh fish ought
For it must have been a week since they'd been caught
But they never told a lie,

They never told a lie
They were Sunday school scholars every one
And they followed in the steps of Washington
And they never told a lie. [10-2-84]

When Marjorie was fourteen, right after her family left the farm to move to the store, she went to Rutland to go to high school. During her first year there she lived with her aunt and her Uncle Clyde (her mother's brother) where she was exposed to a very different kind of music:

Then it was routine duty on Sunday afternoons we'd walk up the railroad tracks and we'd have to go bird hunting. And then when we came back from the bird walk, then we had to sit down in the living room and my uncle would open up the big Victrola and he would play classical music, and he would explain: "Now this is *Aida*." This is the story of so-and-so, and this is John McCormack and he will sing "Kathleen Mavourneen," or a song like that. But most of the music was classical. I can't think of all the names now. And then he would tell the stories of the operas and we would have to listen. And so he was very musically inclined and he liked music the way my mother did. This is one of the songs that he enjoyed singing, and it's called "The Old Refrain:"

THE OLD REFRAIN

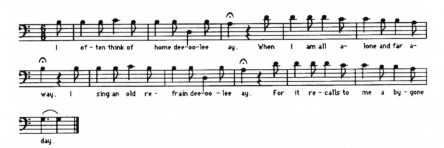

I often think of home dee-oo-lee-ay
When I am all alone and far away.
I sing an old refrain dee-oo-lee-ay
For it recalls to me a bygone day.
It takes me back again to meadows fair
Where sunlight's golden rays beam everywhere.
My childhood joys again come back to me
My mother's face in fancy too I see.
It was my mother taught me how to sing
And to that memory my heart will cling.
I'm never sad and lone while on my way
As long as I as I can sing dee-oo-lee-ay

The years have passed and gone dee-oo-lee-ay
And though my heart is young, my head is gray
Yet still the echoes ring dee-oo-lee-ay
And dear old memories forever stay.
My song can bring me visions full of light
And sweetest dreams throughout the darkest night
Of all that life can give that song is best
I'll take it with me when I go to rest.
And when at last my journey here is o'er
'Twill ring more joyfully than e'er before
For up to heaven I will take my way
The angels too will sing dee-oo-lee-ay

JP: Did your mother ever hear you sing that song, or did you ever hear her sing it?

MP: I never heard her sing it.

JP: Does it seem like the type of song she would sing?

MP: No, it sounds like *his* type--he was very sentimental.[12-1-84]

Marjorie and I talked several times about game songs she knew as a child, but she had some difficulty recalling them. She did report that games were played at school as well as at other times when children and young teenagers gathered together, especially at socials:

JP: Did you ever know a song called "The Needle's Eye?"
MP: Oh yes! Those were games we played at socials, I think. We

used to have socials at different homes and we'd play "Jacob and Rachel," "Drop the Handkerchief," and—Oh, I do recall "London Bridge!" Yes, we did play that. "London Bridge." You're bringing back all these memories that are so far back that I can't remember them.

[spoken]*The needle's eye it does supply*
The thread that runs so truly
It has caught many a smiling one
And now it has caught you. [10-2-84]

Socials were important evening gatherings of neighbors throughout New England. The families that enjoyed music together were also there to help each other during times of need. Socials in which singing and dancing took place also served to expand musical repertoires of the participants beyond their immediate families. Each neighborhood and community had different types of socials. This depended partly on the amount of space available: whether people had large homes, places to shelter horses during a winter event, a dance floor built upstairs in a house, in a barn, or in a town hall or Grange, but also on whether musicians were available:

JP: Can you describe what a social is?
MP: What is a social? Well, in our town of Shrewsbury, a social was held usually at somebody's home—somebody would offer to open their home—mostly some of the younger people would gather together in the evening and they would talk and chat and then they'd decide to play some games and then they would have refreshments. Sometimes the person whose house was being opened up would furnish refreshments. Or more often, each family would bring something like a cake or some sandwiches or what have you.
JP: So the people that came to the social were neighbors—
MP: All neighbors, yes. And some of them would come by horse and buggy or horse and sleigh. But a lot of them right, around in this little area, would walk. I remember that there was a party down on the Cold River Road about a mile from here. And it would be eight or ten people all walked together down to the party and then they would all walk back.[1986]

Another kind of social popular in many neighborhoods throughout northern New England was the kitchen dance or kitchen junket. In the North Shrewsbury area Marjorie reported that kitchen dances were only held once or twice each winter. As she put it, "Dances would be held in the winter—but you could have a social anytime, you know." Marjorie's family did not take part in these social functions as often as they did occasions in which singing was the primary or secondary activity to the occasion:

> I remember only one kitchen dance, and I probably wasn't more than four years old. It was at a farmhouse and my mother and father attended and they put me upon the table in the corner of the room so I wouldn't be in the way, and I looked down upon all these wonderful dancers. I thought it was so interesting. But I didn't take part myself. And then, at the Grange Hall they had entertainment, the townspeople attended and had entertainments and had square dancing. And they must have had some local callers, I don't recollect who they were.[1986]

Public (and semi-public) buildings—such as the Grange, the local church and the schoolhouse—held other events where families sometimes experienced different types of music. When they were very young, Marjorie and her sister were taught songs by their mother so that they could perform at these gatherings:

> **MP**: My mother would teach my sister and me a song. And when we were about—oh perhaps seven, eight, nine, ten years old—she would teach us from some sheet music, or some Christmas songs, and we would sing at Christmas programs, or at Grange meetings, or at Modern Woodman meetings, when there were programs. And we could sing at that time, but of course, I've lost my voice now. My voice is cracked.
>
> But I remember at the Modern Woodman—my father was a Modern Woodman, sort of an Insurance Company—and there was a Modern Woodman meeting at the Grange Hall out at Shrewsbury Center. And my sister and I sang a silly little song:

MY PAPA WAS A WOODMAN
What a pity yours is not
For all the Woodmen are so kind and true
They were so good when Papa died
And all of them have got
A great big heart for little ones like you.

[laughs] Silly. Silly.

MP: Oh, yes, of course it was longer, but that's all I remember. And of course we had Christmas programs at the Northam church. All the families collected and had their Christmas at the church. They didn't have Christmas in the homes in those days. The families took all the presents to the church and we had a big Christmas tree reaching to the roof and there would be a program that the school teacher had arranged and we would have the younger ones—the scholars would sit in the front row and they would recite and sing and have duets—and then there would be older people who sat in the chorus and sang. But the program was essentially put on by the teacher. And we sang Christmas songs. I don't really remember what those Christmas songs were. Just Christmas hymns, I imagine.

And when I was too young to go to school, and couldn't sit in the front row with the school children, I sat in the back with my grandma, my grandma Pierce. And after the program we heard a shout and a tramping and—outdoors on the steps—he said "Oh Ho Ho Ho!" and bells were jingling and this door was flown open and Santa Claus came striding down the aisle and he'd say, "Oh Ho Ho! Merry Christmas! And this is a heavy bag I'm carrying!" And I was frightened. Oh, I was really frightened. And I sat beside grandma, who was a little woman all dressed in black. And my father was probably standing in the back, because the men had to stand in the back, there weren't enough seats for everybody. My mother was probably in the choir. So I got up close to grandma and was so frightened. And she said, "Don't be afraid Marjorie, it's just Uncle Warner." [10-2-84]

Going to Church, 1913. Willie Pierce driving his Morgan horses. Marion, Marjorie, Demaris, Willie and Percy Pierce.

The social sphere for residents of this somewhat isolated community was small. Families worked hard to provide a variety of entertainment during different seasons, especially in winter:

86

MP: When I was young, we had all dirt roads and we didn't have any snow plows. The snow was shovelled by the men in town or we had an old snow roller to pack the roads. And we didn't move around as much as people do now. I rarely went to Cuttingsville, which is four miles away. I did go occasionally to the center where the Town Hall is located for a few events; we had Oyster Suppers and Harvest Suppers—things like that.

JP: Was there music at events like that?

MP: Yes, yes.

JP: What kind of music was it?

MP: Well, there were two girls in town who were called the belles of Shrewsbury and they always sang, and of course we had graduation exercises where we had music, or group music.

JP: Now these songs were different from the songs your mother sang though?

MP: Yes, yes. They would be more modern, if you think 1929 is modern. But these are not modern songs that you have here [referring to her typed texts]. These are 1890's songs, you know, its quite a difference.[1986]

The musical traditions which Marjorie remembers are not actively performed today in her family. Yet Marjorie recalls details of musical events and occasions and frames the role that music and song played in her family's life during the early years of this century. While songs played different roles in the lives of various members of her family, for Marjorie, songs were probably most important as a source of stories:

JP: You talked about the kinds of songs that your various relatives sang, and you talked about Uncle Clyde's songs being sentimental. Can you characterize the kinds of songs that your mother and your grandfather sang?

MP: I think they were just folk songs and most of them had stories. And I think these folk songs—most of them—probably came from England or Scotland—because my mother's background is Scotch Irish. My father's background is English and Dutch. But I think they're just telling little stories as "Margery Grey" tells a story you see. And they just pick them up, and it takes the place of reading a book. Its like reading a book. You pick up a book and it has one type of story and another song has a different type of story. Sometimes there's a happy ending, and often there's a sad ending.

JP: So people that sang those kinds of songs really were story tellers in a way.

MP: I think so. They're what you call folk songs. That's what folk songs are, in my opinion. Just stories.[4-16-85]

****

Family songs and recitations mentioned by Marjorie in interviews between 1984 and 1990:

SONG	SOURCE
Beulah Land	paternal grandfather
Billy Boy	mother
Billy Grimes the Drover (recitation)	mother
The Blackberry Girl (recitation)	mother
Bright Alfarata	mother
Bringing in the Sheaves	
Cabbage and Meat Song (The Half Hitch)	mother
Charley	
Daisy (Daisy Bell)	father
The Faded Coat of Blue	paternal grandfather
Fair Charlotte	mother
The Fox and the Hare	mother/grandfather
The Frog	maternal uncle
The Gypsy's Warning (recitation)	mother
I'll Remember You, Love, in My Prayers	
Johnny Sands (recitation)	mother
Just Before the Battle Mother	paternal grandfather
Learning McFadden to Waltz	
London Bridge	socials
Lord Bateman	mother
Margery Grey	
My Papa Was a Woodman	mother
The Needle's Eye	socials
O My Darling Clementine	mother
Old Dan Tucker	
The Old Refrain	maternal uncle
The Orphan Children	
The Ride of Jenny McNeil (recitation)	mother
The Rose of Tralee	
The Sailor Boy	mother
The Spanish Cavalier	

There is a Tavern in the Town	mother
They Never Told a Lie	
Three Little Kittens (recitation)	
The Two Kittens (recitation)	
Two Little Girls in Blue	
Uncle Ned	
Uncle Tascus and the Dead (recitation)	
We're Tenting Tonight	paternal grandfather
When the Roll is Called Up Yonder	
Whispering Hope	sheet music
The Young Counselor	mother

NOTES

1. The Helen Hartness Flanders Ballad Collection is an archival collection of traditional New England music established by Helen Hartness Flanders of Springfield, Vermont in 1930. Housed at Middlebury College since 1941, it contains over four thousand traditional songs and dance tunes recorded between 1930 and 1960 in all the New England states.

2. "The Half Hitch" was recorded by Flanders in 1932 and published in *Ballads Migrant in New England* (New York: Farrar, Straus and Young, 1953, 33-37) and in *Ancient Ballads Traditionally Sung in New England*, Vol. 1 (Philadelphia: University of Pennsylvania Press, 1961, 266-70); "The Sailor Boy" was recorded in 1932 and the text was published in *The New Green Mountain Songster* (New Haven: Yale University Press, 1939, 39-40); "Lord Bateman" was recorded in 1932 and was published in *Ancient Ballads Traditionally Sung in New England*, Vol. 2 (Philadelphia: University of Pennsylvania Press, 1961, 39-43); "The True Story" was published in *A Garland of Green Mountain Song* (Northfield, Vermont, 1934, 32-33); "The Young Counselor" was published in *Country Songs of Vermont* (New York: G. Schirmer, 1937, 46-47).

3. A version known to Gertrude Spaulding Pierce from her parents Mr. and Mrs. J. K. Spaulding of West Bridgewater. This was sung by Marjorie Pierce to Helen Hartness Flanders in August 1953.

4. Some of these songs are found in collections popular during the late nineteenth century including *Wehman's Collection, Heart Songs, Franklin Square Song Collection*. The Pierces owned both *Heart Songs* and *Wehman's Collection*.

"JUST KEEP THE SAW CUTTING"[1]
by Jane Beck

JOHN'S SHOP

It was a raw, gray day late in October, 1978 when I first found my way into John Lamberton's yard. A classic weatherbeaten Vermont farm house with a wide porch stood hunched over a bend of the Winooski River just outside the village of Marshfield. A few snow flakes suggested we would soon see the first real snow of the season. I climbed the steps to the front door which opened into the kitchen. Hazel Lamberton answered my knock and directed me to a small wooden building in back of the house which served as her husband's shop. I learned later that it had been a hen house he had converted to his needs. He always planned to build a larger one—"if my finances fit my ideas, which they don't a lot of times." [2] (7:10)

John opened the door—a short, bald headed man dressed in green wool pants, suspenders and a plaid shirt. He motioned me into warmth and jumbled chaos. Actually his tools were orderly: his files on the window ledge, his hammers in a neat row, nails in Hills Brothers' coffee cans, saws in a line waiting to be sharpened. A huge ice saw which had been well used in its day hung from the ceiling and dwarfed most of the other objects in his shop, while a couple of newly-finished donut hooks, one of John's own specialties, dangled waiting to be sold—or more characteristically—given to anyone who might stop by. The chaos came from the great assortment of items—mostly old, in various states of disrepair—waiting for a little tinkering to get them back in working order. These cluttered his bench, the walls, the shelves, the floor. Outdated license plates from such states as Alaska, Mississippi, Texas, Florida and Virginia served as a backdrop for the wood stove, while two well-used chairs near it testified to the sociability of the place. Stranger that I was, he motioned me towards the chairs, "Come in and set awhile."

In my role as Folklorist for the Vermont Council on the Arts, I was collecting information on apple lore. Wes Cate, then director of the Vermont Historical Society, had suggested that John would be a wonderful source of information. "He's one of Vermont's originals," he had told me. I explained to John what I was after and he pulled over an old apple peeler that had seen better days. A number of teeth were broken off so that the gears kept slipping. "Maybe a little tinkering could make this work."

A litany of different kinds of apples rolled off his tongue. As a boy he remembered Alexanders, St. Lawrences, Wolf Rivers, Blue Parmeins—a late apple you could get in January and February, Titoskee—an early apple like the Yellow Transparents, Dutchesses, Wealthies, Fameuls, Red Astrachans, Baldwins, Russetts, Pound Sweets and something the old people used to call Sweet Apples—a greenish, yellowish apple the size of a medium Mac. He went on to explain how his grandfather used to store the different apples in bins in the cellar and launched into an anecdote of how one year a squirrel found its way into the cellar. "Gramp" told John and his brother to make a box trap to catch the intruder. This they did and when successful, their grandfather, hoping to have a little fun, took the squirrel up to the kitchen, showed it to the cat and let it go. To the delight of the boys and their grandfather, pandemonium broke loose. But "Gram took a dim view of the proceedings." As John recounted, "It stirred her up some and she warn't too pleased. From then on no squirrels were allowed in the kitchen."

We were launched. During the afternoon I learned that John had been born August 8, 1912 in Cabot. His great-great-grandfather, Nathaniel, "buried right up over the hill here" (2:25) had first come from New Hampshire in 1805 and established the Lamberton family in Vermont. His mother, Victoria, daughter of a stone cutter, came to this country from Italy at the age of two and grew up in the Boston area. She arrived in New Discovery as a school teacher and met John's father, Raymond, at a kitchen junket.[3] They were married in 1910.

John's grandfather, Fred Lamberton, had bought a sawmill in 1906. Raymond had sawed at different mills for over fifty years, thus it was natural that John had an early familiarity with sawmills—the workings of which continued to fascinate him all his life. He held up both hands, wiggling his fingers. "I was lucky. I've still got my thumbs and fingers." His grandfather and father had not been so fortunate:

> The middle finger up to the first joint was the biggest finger Gramp had left on his right hand. Then his thumb on his left hand was gone back to the first joint. Father lost his thumb and index finger on his left hand—off at about the first joint. He did that at seventeen—a little bench saw. He said they was both hanging a little when he went in the house to have his mother cut them off. She wasn't going to so he reached for the shears and then Gram got the shears and snipped them off. Old Dr. Carver sewed him up. He sewed up three generations of us. (1:5)

Wiggling his fingers again, John cautioned, "But I ain't boasting. I could lose some tomorrow in that," pointing to the radial arm saw.

That lead him to discuss mill accidents—but he prefaced his discussion by saying there weren't many. One day when he was sawing a man walked over and held up his hand. Four fingers were missing. John bundled him into the car and drove him to the hospital to be sewed up. Another time he was edging and a second man took over for him while he went to get a drink of water. The board the man was edging was crooked and it somehow snapped back, peeling off his woolen hat and a good part of his scalp. John somehow felt responsible for this accident. Luckily the wound was superficial. Only once had he known of an incident where a man was killed. This occurred in Gorham, New Hampshire—before John had worked there, when a man fell into the saw and was cut in half. But it was not John's nature to dwell on such events, and they only came up in conversation that once.

Throughout his life John had worked in over thirty sawmills. Occasionally when he was out of a job and had to make ends meet he had tried his hand at other things like "drawing granite" or working for a fruit dealer, "but that weren't my line of business at all." (7:16) As he put it, "I most generally found a mill somewhere after a little while." (7:14) He was somewhat wistful as he told me he was the last millman of his family. "None of my boys or any of the rest of them have gone into that." But he was never censorious. He blamed it on the times. "Sawmills are different now. Now the sawyer sets in a little box... all glassed in with plexiglas, sits in a nice easy chair, wiggles a few little things and has two or three things he has to step on to do something else—why!" (1:6)

John's association with a sawmill began at a young age on his grandfather's farm:

> About the first I can remember... I was sawing slabs and you had to put the slabs on this table like... and the handle came up over with a loop in it—up over the saw. I was probably 10-11 years old and I had to jump to reach that handle. Well, one time I missed it and my hand went down onto the saw and it took off my mitten and just scratched my little finger. Just barely scratched it, but it scared me and I told Father I was going up to the house. "Well," he said, "you're all right. Go down and get your mitten, you'll be all right." So I went downstairs and got my mitten. It had cut the back of my mitten just a little and then I went out. I didn't go back upstairs, I went up to the house. (1:1)

The afternoon disappeared and as I made ready to go, I knew I would return. Not only did John tell a good story, but he had something to say. He loved his sawmills and knew them intimately. He respected tradition and the old ways, and was thoroughly schooled in them. He admired continuity and a sense of place and remarked to me a number of times, "Rickers Mill was the oldest mill in the state of Vermont...still in operation, and old Marvin Boomhower sawed there fifty years in the same mill. My father sawed better than fifty years I guess, but not in the same mill." (2:14)

Although John had not gone on to college, he found that his own informal education—one in which he learned by doing, proved just as valuable. At one time or another he had done every job in a sawmill from skidding logs to stacking lumber, and finally to that of sawyer. But he stressed how important it was to learn the more lowly jobs correctly. Stacking lumber had to be done in a particular way—placing the stickers 4 one on top of the other with the front end ever edging slightly forward. Frequently he self-effacingly claimed that the two main requirements of working in a sawmill were a strong back and a weak mind, (10:24) but there was no question that he admired the men who had spent their lifetime in the mill.

He listened carefully to the old stories they told, and passed them on as he had heard them—stretching his knowledge of sawmills back another generation or two:

> Charles Utley, I worked for him a long time, told about this old fellow come to work—quite an old man. Then the logs were all piled up in the winter time and [sawing would] start up in the spring... They'd draw them in at that time with a yoke of oxen. And this old man, quite an old man, came and asked for a job and Charles said, "what do you think you can do?" He said, "Well, I'd like to drive those oxen." Charles said those oxen pulled in the logs as they were sawed. "Do you think you could keep up?" Well, he said he'd like to try. He'd driven oxen and knew what he was talking about and so Charles said he hired him and never had a man that did any better with a yoke of oxen than he did. He'd pull in the logs. He'd have this old big burly log laid out there. They started to get ahead of him a little, he'd bring in that old big log. That would slow them down enough. He never hurried, never hurried. They never ran out of logs, and he was good to the oxen. You couldn't have asked for a better old fellow—but he knew what he was doing. (5:17)

He respected the old timers' wisdom, frequently underscoring their knowledge gleaned from years of doing. "Frank Hemingway was the boss. He was an old mill man. He was a good one. He knew. He'd sawed logs and he *knew*. A lot better to work with somebody like that than somebody graduated from college and got it all out of a book." (3:15) John regretted the demise of the old millmen and said somewhat ruefully, "The old fellows are gone now. Something comes up you want to ask, there isn't anybody that knows. Difference today—[you] don't learn from old people so much, you go to books. And well—half the stuff today isn't worth knowing anyway." (7:8) Yet John was a great reader. He was drawn to history and particularly to books like Robert Pike's *Spiked Boots* and *Tall Trees, Tough Men*. He was fascinated by the Foxfire books and had read the whole series, often drawing parallels to Vermont ways as he knew them.

Throughout his life John had been a retentive listener. He remembered turns of phrase and nuances. When one of the teamsters went to town on a spree, he bragged "bang goes a nickel and a dime ain't nothin'." Or on another occasion, when Orvis Shaw had his pung returned with a broken shaft, Shaw complained emphatically, "Why any woman would have to undergo the agony of suffering the pains of childbirth to bring any such creature as that [the borrower] into this world is more than I can understand." (9:16)

John always underscored the humor of the situation. Understatement was his stock in trade. As a youth he had fired the boiler at a steam mill and it blew up. He described the explosion as a "woof." It "blew the bricks out of the back end of the boiler. Blew the boards out of the end of the mill... A good size woof, maybe." (1:4) Or when he worked for Nate Flint for twenty years, it was time enough to "get acquainted." (1:15) His expressions were colorful and descriptive. Men living in logging camps were fed "beans and flapjacks and teas strong enough to float an axe." (10:15) And when you sawed with water power, "you had to use it because it didn't go by but once, you know." (10:10)

From these years of listening, John had perfected his story telling techniques. He strung words together in a memorable and evocative way. Because of this ability he served for several years as town moderator, and when two of his daughter's were graduating from high school and at the last minute the principal couldn't be there for the ceremony, his daughter Denise came up to him in the audience and said, "Mr. Burbank can't make it. Can you M.C. the program for us?" John saved the day and delighted his audience as well. As his wife Hazel said, "That was right up his alley."

As John approached the end of his life he still maintained a lively curiosity in the world around him. He told about a place where the Indians had raised and ground corn. He had drawn logs by it for years and then one day when he was travelling around, "just for fun," his companion had showed him the hole where the corn had been ground. He was interested in everything—from the making of cedar oil to the growing of ginseng as a cash crop. He kept up with the times, but he found it difficult to comprehend some of the changing attitudes that came with newer lifestyles. He believed in individual freedoms and didn't approve of the encroachment of government in this area. While today the government seems to be into everything, "Back then a fellow could run his own business." (1:14) And he certainly did not approve of our throwaway culture. His shop was an affirmation to that fact. Frequently he would mention as an aside, "Them days they used to fix things." He'd shake his head in wonderment. "They take the dumps away from us and then make things to throw away." (2:11)

Although he commented on his grandfather's disdain of time, "time don't mean anything to me," John was not enthralled with the modern day pace, yet paid begrudging lip service to the axiom, "Go modern or go broke." He steadfastly resisted going modern, clinging to his old values which served him well. "Oh, there used to be a lot of good folks. I guess there is now, but they don't have time to do those things or don't take the time." John took the time. Anyone who stopped by was always welcomed, always treated to warm hospitality. If John was in his shop, he would stop his tinkering, pull up a chair and go to visiting. Always when the individual left, it was, "Don't forget to come back."

RECORDING HIS LIFE STORY

I met John Lamberton at a time when as he put it, "I kind of like to remember" and when I was hungry to listen and absorb. I realized what a wealth of information he held in his head—information that could not be found in any books. He was modest about his knowledge—"don't know too much," and unlike many people who relate their life story over time, he never promoted himself. "When I say I sawed so much of something, don't get the idea that I did it alone, because I didn't. Had six or seven men helping me all the time. And I don't think I done anything that somebody hasn't already done or will do." (1:18)

In November I stopped back to see John and broached the idea of recording his life story. My job at the Arts Council was to discover through fieldwork, what traditional ways still existed in Vermont. Certainly logging and sawmills were a large part of Vermont tradition and here was a man who could tell me about them. He was agreeable and warmed to the thought as he explained to me that the story of a sawmill should be related from

96

the ground up, rather than from the perspective of the man at the top. John never owned his own mill. As he told Nate Flint who was complaining about having to pay his men's social security, withholding, and workman's compensation, "If you didn't have to, I'd have a little mill of my own somewhere." He recalls Nate looking him right in the eye and responding, "God damn you, you know more than I thought you did!" (1:15)

We started in earnest on December 6th. I arrived to find John in the kitchen surrounded by photographs. We poured through these at the kitchen table, as he explained to me about the workings of a sawmill. I needed educating. I had been in and out of sawmills from time to time, but I knew next to nothing of their internal workings. John was patient with my questions and clear with his descriptions, often returning to his photographs to illustrate a point. Later he took me to a number of mills and showed me first hand. He enjoyed talking and easily filled both sides of a 90 minute tape.

Our habit was to sit at the kitchen table. I came every week, usually around two or three in the afternoon and would stay for a couple of hours or so—long enough to complete a tape with some time for visiting on either side. These tapes were transcribed, and I brought the transcripts to John who went over them carefully, making corrections, filling in names, and generally checking their content to his satisfaction. I would enter his corrections on my copy.

Over the next four months I recorded John Lamberton's life story, but that was just the beginning. For the ensuing eight years we toured the countryside, visiting sawmills run by both water power and electricity, and a cedar oil still. We sampled a variety of sugaring operations—from those using oxen and horses to the most modern, state-of-the-art sugar house with two enormous evaporators. We watched men skidding logs with horses, we attended the Danville Fair, we witnessed Orion Dunn boring pump logs, and we talked with innumerable people. Always on these trips there would be a running commentary from John in the car. He had become my teacher in earnest and we both enjoyed it. If too much time went by before I found my way to his door, he would call to tell me of some tantalizing thing we had to do. It was always fun and I always learned something.

We shared the curse of being diabetic and often on our outings we would sneak off like two kids playing hooky from school, and have a piece of homemade pie at the Village Restaurant in Hardwick. He gave me some Jerusalem artichokes telling me that they were good for people "who had sugar." He warned me, "they'll grow worse than witchgrass, you know... Used to be the old folks always had artichokes, a patch, you know around. Sit by the fire in the evening, munch on an artichoke, shell beans or something. That's one of the old old things." (5:12)

Today, every time I come up our driveway I smile and remember as I pass an ever-expanding crop of artichokes that has exploded over the bottom of our garden. Green in the summer, they tower as brown sentinels above the snow in winter. I treasure the legacy.

THE EARLY YEARS

John's first memories are of the farm in Cabot. "Gramp was the farmer," he said. It was a small farm with a few cows, pigs, sheep, poultry and a sawmill.

John's grandfather was a jack-of-all trades. One winter he blacksmithed at Lanesboro while his wife cooked, and his son sawed chair stock. He also had been in partnership with his brother. Together they owned horses and travelled about with horsepower,[5] sawing wood and pressing hay. By the time they dissolved their partnership John's grandfather had gone into the mill business. It was then he bought a water powered mill up by Marshfield Dam, or as it is known today, Molly's Falls Pond. He changed it over, putting in a boiler and a steam engine. Shortly after, it burned and with no insurance, Fred Lamberton was forced into bankruptcy. This was not an uncommon occurrence. A number of steam powered mills burned in those years. With the dry sawdust one spark would set it afire. Usually the engine could be saved. As John said, "Couldn't hurt the engine very much... They might take the babbit out of the bearings... They'd take a little tinkering, you know, but was cheaper than buying a new one. Them days they used to fix things." So when John was about four, his grandfather moved to the farm in Cabot and placed the steam engine beside a brook from which he could draw water for the boiler.

We had the sawmill—used to have our own meat and potatoes and raised oats for the horses. I can remember there was a little granary we called it. One year we had this field of Northern corn—that you'd let ripen and then pick it and husk it, took it down to the grist mill, ground it. Fed it to the pigs. Used to raise quite a few pigs and sold them. We butchered our own—had our own slaughter house: beef, pigs. I remember having sheep, but I don't know as they ever butchered any sheep. I can remember shearing them all by hand—send the wool and it came back in them little rolls. (5:2)

In those days there was no electricity on the farm. "We had one of those gasoline Coleman lanterns out in the barn," (9:3) and everything was done with horses—haying, spreading manure, skidding logs and drawing lumber. "I remember one old horse we had—skidding logs. I've seen her go along and the end of the log would hit something. She'd swing right square around, take a couple of steps, pull the log away from whatever and then come back into the skidding trail. Nobody said a word to her at all. Old Nancy her name was. She was a good one, just a little morgan horse." (8:21)

In John's earliest years they also had oxen:

My father always said he'd rather skid logs with an ox than a horse—that's pulling them from the tree around to the pile. But he said an ox would plow right through the snow while a horse jumped. He said the chain used to get dirty behind the ox once in awhile... I can just remember the old red ones we had and then after that we had a yoke of holstein oxen. (8:21)

John went on to describe the farm as it lingered in his mind's eye:

I remember Gramp milking. They used to have five cows and Gram would milk four while Gramp would milk one with one hand. I said something about I'd think you'd go crazy or something. "Time don't mean nothing to me," he'd tell me and sit there milking. (2:9)

Under one barn there was a sheep pen and under the other barn was the duck pen. A few chickens just for eggs. Gram used to have turkeys. The old turkey would go and steal a nest out in the woods and we'd have to go and find her, tie a rag on the bush. Then when they'd hatch, more trouble than cows or horses—little turkeys out in the wet grass--have to go and find them. And hens with their chicks. I can remember Gram cussing at them. Some of them in the house and then they'd go around with their beak open. Used to feed them gun powder.[6] I can remember Gramp taking apart the shot gun shells. Gram would have them in a towel on her lap, spoon the gun powder in. Not enough to blow them up! I can remember butchering—Gramp making sausage in a washtub. About two-thirds full, stirring it. Mixed up all this and that—ground up all the meat. Different spices, sage ...but I can remember him with his stub hands stirring it in the washtub. Set on the stove—maybe a little fire. Then they'd put it in bags. (5:2-3)

Uncle Harry, Gram's brother was both the butcher and teamster on the farm. He was known as a good horseman and "he was the boss when we were butchering. Soak the hams and bacon and then have a barrel out on the lawn covered up and hang in there and smoke them." (4:5) Uncle Harry was a favorite with the younger generation and used to come driving into the yard with his horse and buggy, unhitch his horse, put her in the barn and stay for a week, two weeks or a month. Then one day he would hitch up again and drive off. He was John's drinking uncle and although he never over-indulged while he stayed, his nephews were aware that when there was hard cider in the cellar, Uncle Harry needed to go down to check the furnace pretty often. Perhaps it was these trips that led John to comment dryly that he was "a little allergic to work."

In those days of the small self-sufficient farm, the family was at the hub of the universe:

Thanksgiving, Christmas, we'd get together... I remember one time up on the farm—the great big table... there must have been more than twenty of us. Uncle Coolidge came from New Discovery, Uncle Slayton from East Calais, he ...married one of my grandfather's sisters—two or three of them came. And I can remember.. Gram had two chicken pies—made in the old milk pans, the round ones. And then in the middle of it she'd have the big earthen mug bottom side up to hold the crust up—gory that was good. Dressing, squash, potatoes, most all home-grown. (9:8)

Throughout his life, John maintained close links with all his family. Until his father retired from sawing in 1956, they usually worked as a team, Raymond sawing, John working behind him on the edger. In turn John became the patriarch of his own family, which today numbers six children, sixteen grandchildren and an ever growing number of great-grandchildren.

There were two houses on his grandfather's farm:

> One big house where Gramp and Gram lived and down across the yard was a smaller house where my father and mother and us kids—three of us were born up there—and we lived down in the other house. And Gramp and Gram lived up in the big house and kept the mill help—the hired man—always had one or two hired men all the time and then when we were sawing and logging in the winter, more. Some of them came from neighbors right around. Hubert Wheeler, I remember, lived up on the hill there. He used to work down in the mill. In the spring it would be muddy when we was sawing and he used to wear his rubber boots and had a pair of shoes down in the mill. And he'd stick his feet into them and start. Well, somebody put a spike down through each one of them and the next morning when he slipped his feet in and started, he didn't go. He was mad—he couldn't take a joke. I think he quit for a while. But he came back. Wavie Sulham fired the boiler—he was shoveling off the roof one winter and it settled down with him. Didn't hurt him. That was an old old fashioned mill. They aren't made like that now. Sawed a lot of lumber. (1:20)

John's introduction to sawmills came early in life. By the time he was fifteen or sixteen he was sawing shingles. He remembers his grandfather urging, "Just keep the saw cutting, my boy. That's all there is to it," which as John commented "is saying quite a lot without talking too much." (2:8) They would saw shingles after they finished sawing logs. At that time they would set up the shingle machine in the sawmill.

> In the summertime Grandfather would fire the boiler and my brother and I would saw shingles... (1:3) Get over there in the morning—Curt and I, we'd have to milk first... and then we'd get over to the mill—oh, half-past eight, eight o'clock, and Gramp would have steam up and all ready. If we had enough blocks all cut up we'd saw forty bunches that day. Then we had the logs. We had a circular saw set up to cut the logs into blocks 16 inches long. Lots of time we'd have to do that. But forty bunches was pretty good—for boys, you know, and Gramp—you got to figure Gramp. (1:15)

> Gramp would fire the boiler [with the sawdust.] That worked awful good because you got rid of all the sawdust and waste from the

saw which is a problem today. One of us—my brother and I—one would saw a while,... then we had to pack them up into the bunches... We'd swap back and to. Sometimes we'd get to visit. The shingle mill was up one floor... [the] engine was down on the ground on a cement base of course and then the shingle mill was up. We'd get to talking and then Gramp would come out under and thump the floor with the hoe handle. "Keep the saw cutting, boys!" he'd say. He used to say that once in awhile. (1:2)

Even at this young age, John's life cycle followed the seasonal rhythm of the sawmill. Years ago, they didn't saw in winter. That was the time to get the logs out. Sawing began when it thawed:

We'd go into the woods and start cutting logs in the fall before snow—get the roads built and the swamp holes corduroyed. That's putting logs across the road close together, be sure and leave them apart far enough so that if the horse's foot went down through you could pull it out. Then put on brush and then when you got snow it would be all right. When you got snow enough we'd start drawing the logs out to the mill and piling them up and in the spring when it begun to thaw out and got nasty and muddy and everything, then we'd start sawing. A lot of the old mills were like that. (1:2)

John attended school in Cabot. In the early years he rode with a neighbor but the year he was a freshman in high school his brother Bob went into the eighth grade and together they drove their own horse. "Now the bus goes up there," (1:14) John stated dryly.

John finished high school in 1930 and was eager to go to work in a sawmill. He commented to me that his two brothers and sister had gone on in school. Curt became a school teacher, Bob a mine foreman, while his sister, Teresa, was a registered nurse. As he put it, "They all got educated but me. I went to work for a sawmill. My folks wanted me to go to college, but I wanted to get into that sawmill. I don't know that I'd swap with any of them if I had it to do over." (1:6) Although John may not have received a "formal" higher education, he studied and absorbed a unique curriculum on the job. It proved to be a sound and extensive education in people and in wood.

UTLEY'S MILL

After high school, John went to work for Charles Utley. "He was kind of a funny old fellow—a mind of his own." (10:10)

> Utley's mill was right up near West Hill Pond. That's the first mill I ever worked in besides our own. I used to run the edger quite awhile. That's taking the boards away from the big saw and putting them through this machine that has two saws that takes the bark off each side of the board. Done different things there—that was a steam mill. I used to fire the boiler some. One day I was firing I remember, and one of the tubes busted in the boiler inside. It was probably four feet in diameter, and then inside is these plates in the end with holes and tubes going from one end to the other for the fire to go through. Well, one of them broke out in the back end of it. So we had to hoe the fire out and get a new one and put it in, and away we went again. It didn't hurt anybody. [There was] a woof, kind of—blew the boards out of the end of the mill, kind of. A good size woof, maybe. (1:3)

There were eight or nine men working for Utley at the mill. John ticked them off: the fireman, (who fired the boiler) the turner, "he rolls the logs (on the carriage) behind the sawyer," the sawyer, the edger man, and "two or three men out in the back end and some more stacking lumber and another man pulling in logs with horses from the piles out in the yard on a little scoot." [7](1:4)

Charles Utley was a good business man and had his finger in a number of enterprises. John worked for him for several years in a variety of capacities. During the summer while his father sawed, John stacked the maple planking that during the winter they made into lawn mower handles. For two or three winters John and his father boarded above Utley's food and grain store in Hardwick, while working in his shop. Commenting on this period John recalled, "I thought we'd made lawnmower handles enough for the world." (1:16)

One day John was working at Utley's mill when Charles Utley appeared during the noontime dinner break:

> Charles said, "When're you getting done here?" "Well, we'll probably finish up today." "Well, I want you to come with me. I just bought another truck and I want you to drive it. And I want to do something with it this afternoon so I won't have to start using it on a Friday." [8] He wouldn't start anything on Friday—never. And he had

enough to do. So Charles took me over to Hardwick and got the truck and I went out and got a load of gravel. Stone chips down to the stoneshed and brought them over to Cabot to build the new Masonic Hall. So we done something with it and the next day we went to drawing logs. (10:12)

Charles Utley also supplied a great deal of lumber and John, with a second man, Chauncy Clark drove Utley's trucks for a period of time. One long day found them in Vergennes at six in the evening stacking four-inch novelty siding. It was close to ten o'clock when they drove into Utley's yard in Hardwick. He came out, as he always did. "Have any trouble, boys?" "No, just took a little time to stack that four-inch lumber." His only comment was, "I thought maybe it would." (10:13)

LOGGING CAMPS

In the winter of 1936 and '37, John and his father went to work for Fairbanks and Morse where they continued, seasonally for the next five years. Their boss was Arthur Sanborn whom John described as a hard worker. Arthur never swore and was "an awful nice old fellow." There was never a written agreement, but every summer Sanborn would let them know if he needed them for the coming year. The company had a piece of land on Walden Mountain. The boarding house on it had been built about the time of the Civil War and Fairbanks had logged up there since then.

The teamsters would start cutting logs in the fall, before the snow. This work was done with horses and when the snow came, they would draw the logs down to the mill. Sometimes these loads would be considerable. "Up on the mountain Jim Hayes and his team, Tom and Jerry, they came in with a little over 2000 feet of logs once. That's pretty good for a pair of horses... Big horses. They were big. Old Tom weighed a ton." (4:5)

The mill men would go into operation around New Year's and begin sawing. They would saw until the roads broke up in the spring, returning in June when they could get the trucks up to the mill and take out the rest of the sawed lumber as well as the slabs which they would draw to St. Johnsbury and Burlington to burn instead of coal.

John and his father would go to work during the week between

Christmas and New Year's to get the mill prepared—line it up, level the track that the carriage went on, and put the belts on the machinery. Bill Spencer, the man who fired the boiler, would start the fire and get the engines ready to begin sawing. "Old Bill knew steam engines—he used to be an engineer on the railroad up in Canada. Part of one foot was gone—railroad accident... But he knew steam engines... he used to get me to help him once in a while. He was a pretty good old fellow." (1:18-19)

It was here that John and his father first worked as a team, John running the edger behind his father, the sawyer. As in all sawmills there was a good deal of practical joking and John had a good memory for these kinds of incidents:

> There were two of us behind the saw. One sawed slabs and the other run the edger. I run the edger and the other fellow sawed slabs. He was a good old fellow—a little space to rent upstairs, put it that way, but a good old worker. The boys would pick on him some. He had this big piece of a belt that he'd tie—a string went around his waist and that hung down by his legs so when the slabs went by they wouldn't scrape his overalls or pants. This big string to go around him—well, he'd throw it on this table of the slabsaw when he went to dinner and it got so—well, two or three times the boys tied that string so when Ed went to pick it up, it didn't come. So after that he'd wear it right home to dinner. He didn't take it off at all. Another time the handle that he pulled up on—the saw came up through the rolls there. Well, all of a sudden he said to me, "that log must have a lot of pitch on it." He showed me his glove. It was all gooey. Went along, went along and a few minutes Ed says, "I found out where that pitch was coming from. The boys dropped a mess of grease on the bottom of that handle. They must get a kick out of wasting grease like that." (8:7)

The logs were brought into the mill on a carriage which ran on tracks: first the rounded part of the log—the slabs were cut off. These were then sawed into four foot pieces, hauled out of the mill in a cart, removed by hand and dumped into a pile which would then be taken to St. Johnsbury and burned in the summertime. After the slab had been removed from the lumber, it went through the edger which took off a narrow piece of bark, known as "edgings." These were piled on another cart which carried them to the end of the mill, where they would be dumped off. During the wintertime, these were burned. Because of the fire hazard, in the summer, they would extend the track and leave the edgings in a pile to be burned over Christmas when the men first went up to ready the mill. Once through the edger, the log went to the sawyer who was considered the main man in the sawmill. "If the sawyer stopped, everything stopped." (11:16) The sawyer's job was to get the maximum number of boards out of the log. When the log was sawed into boards, the lumber was brought out on another cart, neatly piled up and then loaded on to teams of horses who would draw it down to North Danville. Once there, the lumber would be loaded into trucks and taken to St. Johnsbury.

The millmen began work at 7:00 and finished at 5:00. Then it was the night watchman's job to clean up the mill, take the ashes out of the fire box, and clean the boiler, which meant blowing out the tubes. If they were extremely dirty, these tubes would be brushed first. The night watchman was on duty all night, and in the morning he would have the steam hissing in the boiler.

John and his father lived in the boarding house. One year there were thirty-two boarders—both teamsters and millmen. Jim Hayes, boss of the logging, also ran the boarding house while his wife did most of the buying for it. Board was ninety cents a day, with bed and mattress provided, although the men had to furnish their own bedding. As John says, "I never knew of any bedbugs or lice up there," however at other camps they were not so fortunate. The second floor housed the sleeping quarters. John and his father shared a room and a large bed. Downstairs was the mess, where the men ate at big long tables and the bar room which was an all-purpose room. Another name for this was the ram's pasture—with the old washboiler full of water on the big box stove. "That's where you got the hot water to shave your face. Friday nights was shaving nights. Pretty good-looking crew around there Saturday." (10:18) The ram's pasture was also where the deacon's seat was. "One old fellow, he'd talk and talk and talk. He wouldn't get done storytelling or whatever it was, but he'd start right in tomorrow night after supper right where he left off. Nobody had a chance to say anything. But he's gone now. By gory, most of them have." (1:14) They also used to play such card games as 63 and

100 pede and cribbage. John recalls Jim Hayes coming in and watching for a few minutes and then saying "Fifteen-two, fifteen-four, go! I've got to go and give fifteen to those horses." (10:16)

The cook started the day earlier than most and seldom took part in the activities after supper. He would do the dishes and go to bed:

> Boy, we got food. Baked beans on the table three times a day. But plenty of meat and potatoes. Beef butts they were. Now I don't know what part of the beef they were but some of them were kind of tough. One time this old fellow was sawing away with his knife at his plate and he said, "They must have killed this old bull with a harness on and I've got a piece of the britchen." But it was good solid meat, homemade bread, oatmeal, chocolate pies—lot of chocolate pies. Not too big a pie. But the best thing I remember about that cook was he didn't know there were more than four pieces in a pie. Which many times at night I've eaten a whole one after supper. But you could eat then, you know. (1:10)

He'd stay up there three, four, five months and then he'd go down to St. Johnsbury. Be gone four-five days, come back up, and he'd been on a bat, I'd say. His face was purple and he'd go around through the rooms and anything anybody had in their bags or anything in a bottle that would run out, he'd drink it. I used to have Absorbine Jr.—one shoulder bothered me a little—but he'd drink that. I don't know if there was any alcohol in it or not, but I supposed it warmed him up some. But he got straightened out after a few days and be all right. (1:11)

Everyone would work until "the sledding broke up" and then many of the millmen went to Danville to hire on at Harry Davis's of Danville Manufacturing Company. As John put it, Harry Davis was a man who "could explain things quite plainly." (11:8) He could "rave and swear something terrible... but he was a pretty good fellow." (1:13) Davis had a couple of mills and would transport the men where he needed them.

During this period, John boarded in Danville. There were a number of millmen as well as a smattering of other boarders including Hazel Hatch, who lived there during the week with her

**Delbert Cilley (left) and Jack MacPherson returning
to the Walden mill after dumping a load of edgings,
winter, 1938-39.**

aunt who ran the boarding house. Hazel worked in St. Johnsbury
in the Production Credit Association. This was the beginning of
John and Hazel's courtship. As the millmen finished at five, they
would eat in a group at 5:30. Everyone else had supper at 6:00.
Then sometimes she and John would go into St. Johnsbury to the
movies. They were married December 24, 1938.

John and his father sometimes worked as a team to build a
sawmill. They built one for the Beede boys, as John called them in
Hardwick the summer of 1938. During the 1938 hurricane the top
and the sides of the building fell over and had to be put back. The
hurricane blew down a vast amount of timber and sawmills sprang
up everywhere. There was a lot of lumber for sale and nobody
wanted to buy it, so the government stepped in and bought it. This
caused a new brand of individual to appear at the mill. "Young
fellows who'd been to school for a couple of weeks who knew all
about lumber." This "book learning" did not always sit well with
the old timers. During this period John occasionally worked for the
Beede boys:

> I remember one time over to Hardwick I was working at this
> Beede's and Lester Bickford—he was an old, old millman and I think
> he had a government job, scaling... These young fellows used to come
> and you had to keep each kind of wood separate, like maple or rock
> maple and birch and all the different kinds. Well, this young fellow,
> he'd been there quite a while. He thought he knew quite a lot more than

Lester figured he knew. One day he said to Lester, "How do you tell the hard maple from the soft maple?" Lester said, "I kick the end of the log good and hard. If it hurts my foot it's hard maple."... Another time this fellow was sawing, Bill Morrison. He was an old good sawyer—and the back end of the mill was full of those [government] fellows. Must of been six or seven of them out there. I was running the edger and Bill motioned to me and I went over. He said, "Do you think President Roosevelt's in that bunch out in the back end of the mill?" I told him I didn't know and he said, "I'd wished you'd make sure cause for years I've wanted to shake hands with him." (6:9)

Whether college graduate or not, the greenhorn in the mill served as a butt of humor for the more experienced workers. They would send him looking for nonexistent materials such as "sky hooks" or a log stretcher. "Where's that log stretcher? Well the last time you know they had it was up to Orange."

STOVEPIPE CITY

During the hurricane Fairbanks and Morse, who had a two-mile square tract of land over in Lyman, New Hampshire, lost a great number of trees. In order to save the lumber, they had to saw it up:

They had a sawmill over there—the carriage and boiler and engine piled up together in an old shed. We went over there in the fall and built the boarding house first. And the loggers were there. This boarding house was eighteen feet by thirty-six feet. And what I'm getting at is the bedroom upstairs was one great, big open room and sixteen of us was sleeping up there. And you wake up in the night and you'd hear lots of different kinds of noises. But we built the boarding house and then we built the sawmill and got the boiler and engine set up. (1:11)

That was steam—boiler and engine. We had to go way up in the woods to a little boiler. Dam up the brook and then we run a pipe from there down to a big tank in the mill for the water in the boiler. (1:12)

And then we went back up on the mountain [Walden] and sawed out what logs were up there. Must have sawed them all. I guess they didn't cut as much that year knowing they had this over to [Lyman] cause we took some of the machinery from Walden Mountain over to Lyman and started that next summer I guess. I wasn't there when they first started. I don't know how I happened not to be. But I was over to Danville Fair the 8th of August—my birthday—and I saw Arthur [Sanborn] and he wanted to know if I wouldn't come over there and run the edger. Then they were working two shifts. One shift started at 3 A.M. and got done around noon and the other started at around noon and got done around 9 at night. And he wanted me to work the second shift and run the edger. So I went over, built a camp. Then I had my wife and oldest daughter—she was about a year old. I think my camp was fourteen by sixteen we lived in that winter. Then the next summer I built another room on to it. We sawed there sixteen months—two shifts. Then the last six months we had just one shift. Sawed some over eight million feet.

That was a very good job... There was twenty some camps around—children, school bus went through there, grocery man came around and took orders. It was quite a little village. (1:12

The men jokingly called the camps "Stovepipe City."

It was the fall of 1939 when John joined the crew. His father and John's two brothers, Curt and Bob, who served as mill hands, stacking lumber and removing slabs and edgings, were already working.

Curt was full of fun and christened the community outhouse "Pinehurst". This was located half-way between the boarding house and the mill. It was a fair-sized outhouse—as outhouses go, erected over a slit trench in the ground. There were no holes inside. Just a long board about chair high to sit on. When one slit trench was filled the men would dig another, pick up "Pinehurst" and move it on to a new one, while covering up the old. There were always men who liked to "give" a joke but couldn't take one. Such a man was Delbert Cilley who was the foreman of the day shift. He was a good man but known to be extremely lazy. Curt was quite a prankster and the last time "Pinehurst" was moved John's brother picked out a large pine slab, inscribed the words, "Here lies the body of Delbert Cilley" and planted it very firmly and conspicuously over the spot that "Pinehurst" had just vacated:

While John built his own camp, he and his brother Bob lived in a tent off their father's camp. John said of his own lodging. 'Twarn't too big and I boarded off the ceiling and papered it and [it was] snug as a bug in a rug. Got a load of sawdust and put the old fashioned banking clear around. Had a window right in front of the sink and I dug a hole out aways and then put the sink spout out so we didn't have to carry out the water. There was this big maple tree there and I had a birdfeeder

110

hung on a wire. Used to put donuts out in it. This red squirrel, I don't know if it was the same one, come and he'd work and work and finally he'd go up the tree and out a limb and down around under into that birdfeeder, pick up the donut and drop it out over the side and then go back up the tree and onto the ground and take the donut and go away with it. Hazel had a lot of fun watching it. (6:13)

Once he had built his camp, John was joined by his wife and young daughter. With Hazel there, John had the luxury of home cooked food. He had half an hour for dinner between 5:00 and 5:30. "Hazel would have it right on that table, on my plate pretty near, when I got there, cause I didn't have too much time." (10:20) His grandfather's lesson on how to make a box trap to catch the squirrel stood John in good stead. He built another to catch rabbits and this way he and Hazel would supplement their usual bill of fare.

John not only ran the edger but at least twice a day he filed it to keep it sharp. He also filed the big boardsaw at night, "so Father would have a sharp one for morning." (10:21) This was something his father had shown him—just once:

> He'd take the swedge, that's a little tool, and put it on the tooth and hit it to knock the corners of the teeth. Well, it sets it, in other words. To make where the saw cuts wider than the saw so the saw don't rub. Those little corners got to be out there... One side of the swedge is rounded so it makes each corner go out and then the other side is straight. You turn it around and then put that on and hit and that straightens the top of the tooth. Then you file the bottom and just brush the top a little. Father did that and he said, "I want you to make them look just like that." And he laid the file down and went off. That was my session of knowing how to file a saw. I got it after awhile. (10:21)

GORHAM, NEW HAMPSHIRE

In 1951 John had the opportunity to take a job over in Gorham, New Hampshire with Johnson's Lumber Company. This proved to be the largest mill he ever worked at with its 300 horsepower steam engine. "Oh a good one, it run everything." (1:7) He worked there for two years, the first winter he boarded by himself. The next year his family joined him. "Hazel could stand at the sink washing dishes and see me (working) right down there. Had to kind of tend to business." (1:7) As at Lyman, there were two shifts of men sawing.

Every so often the hot pond where the logs were floated to keep them clean would begin to stink and would have to be cleaned out. In the winter the steam exhaust from the engine would go into the pond so that it wouldn't freeze. "The little old French fellow that turned for me on the carriage, come dinner time and the little pond would be pretty rank. Leo Chibeau, his name was. Leo would say, 'Well, John, I guess I won't go down on the beach and have dinner today.' Then we'd clean it out." (3:13) This was not a pleasant job. Not only did the pond stink, but the water had to be drained by hand, with buckets, dumped into a big oil drum, and then put into a truck. It was usually on a Saturday:

> Friday night the boss said, "We're going to clean the pond tomorrow, Louis, will you be here?" He always called him Louis. Leo said, "Well, I will if nothing happens." Didn't see him. Monday morning I kind of sided up to him and I said, "Something happen Saturday, Leo?" He said, "Yes, my wife and I went to Niagara Falls." He was a good old fellow.
>
> I pinched my finger one day--good shape in the sawyer's favorite--that's the dog that holds the logs. There's hooks on the top and the bottom and then you turn this handle and it brings them together. And oh, I pinched my finger. I was blessing the sawyer's favorite and everything else and Leo leaned over and he said, "I always wondered what you called that thing, John, but I didn't want to ask you. Afraid you'd think I was nosey." (3:13)

It was at Gorham that John sawed his biggest log. He explained that sometimes it would take two hours to saw a log that was thirty inches in diameter because the saw wouldn't reach up through and it would be necessary to chop down:

> I guess the biggest log I ever sawed was a maple log over to Gorham—forty-two inches. But there I had one saw right atop of the other one so I didn't have to chop. There was a maple and a birch and I think there was a little over twelve hundred feet in those two logs. I think one was eight feet and one was ten feet. But a log twelve feet long, forty inches in diameter would scale eight hundred feet... I've sawed them thirty inches with just one saw—that's four hundred and fifty feet. Takes a little fussing, rather not have them quite so big. (5:17)

THE FLINT BROTHERS

When John finished at Gorham, he returned to Vermont and went to work in Barre for the Flint brothers, Nate and Jake—where his father was already sawing. He continued with them for the next twenty years.

"That was a good place to work." (1:10) John commented. The brothers had their differences and as John put it, "If one said it was black the other said it was white before he looked at it even. It was too bad. Why they could have been millionaires time and time again, the business they had." (1:10)

The Flints had a number of mills all run by steam. Unlike some of the larger mills that John had worked at the boiler would not be fired all night. Instead a man would come around five A.M. and have the steam ready to start at seven. "If he didn't Nate would explain to him that he should have." (2:12) John remembers that Ervin Clark, "the old boss down in Barre was good to us. He said if it ever got too cold we wouldn't saw. One morning it got down to thirty below zero and we sawed just the same so we never knew. It never got too cold." (1:6)

John went on to explain that once in awhile when it was that cold the pipes would freeze, and he described how they had a hose they could hitch to the boiler to thaw them out. He continued, "you have to move right around in the morning when it's thirty below anyway. 'Twasn't too bad in the mill itself. The big door was open where the logs came in up this slip... but all the rest of the mill was closed up and the boiler in this mill was down to the other end. We didn't get much heat from the boiler." (1:6)

To keep warm the men wore felt shoes and overshoes and wool clothing:

> The last I got, the best, were Navy surplus overalls. Wool.. Oh, them were warm... Good wool mittens, then the leather outside. Them worked pretty good. Three or four pair, then you could have some in drying and getting warm. And the teeth that go in the saw, little bits of things, I used to keep them in on the boiler cause you couldn't put them on with mittens on. Nate always said, "You'd ought to have a place to file saws in by the boiler there." Well, I said I didn't want one by the boiler there. Go in there and get all undressed, or else work with your clothes on and get all covered with sweat and then go out and you're

Fairbanks and Morse Sawmill in Lyman, N.H., 1939.

cold. Do it out in the cold. I used to keep the hammer and sledge and teeth and stuff all in on the boiler where they were warm. (7:18)

John's father sawed at Flints for a number of years before he finally retired in the fall of 1957. Nate asked John if he could carry on:

> I said, "I guess so. But I don't want to saw, Nate. But I'll try to keep it going until you find somebody." "Well, he said, "I know you will, go ahead." So I started sawing. One day a couple of men came in there. I don't know how long this was after I started sawing. But these two men came in and stood awhile. They didn't say anything to me. Went out. I never saw anybody else that I thought was interested. Run along into February and it was going pretty good. I was getting along pretty good. So I told the mill boss, "Going pretty good, Ervin. I don't know but I'd just as soon saw." So he said, he'd tell Nate. So the next day Ervin come over and he said, "I told Nate what you said." I said, "What'd he say?" He said, "Tell him to keep sawing." So I kept sawing. (1:15)

Flints was a good size operation with twenty-five men in the woods, in the shop and in the mill. Although John stayed in the mill he knew all of the men who worked in the woods.

Many of these men worked with the Flints for a considerable length of time and knew each other's weaknesses and foibles. Carl St. John who was boss of the woods for Flint, was frightened of thunderstorms and lightning. They would use a horse to bunch the logs into small bunches of three or four hundred feet and then the tractor would pull the bunches out. Sam Beede drove the tractor.

John Lamberton's camp, Lyman, N.H., fall, 1939.

One day they had quite a thunderstorm and Carl was scared to death. Sam said, "By God, Carl, we'll have Nate put lightning rods on to you and then you'll be all right... I don't know about him ever getting the lightning rods, but that was one solution they figured out. Then they had this shanty—probably about 8 feet wide by 10 or 13 feet long—on big skids that they could take around in the woods to eat dinner in. And one day, this Sam, he was a character anyway—the stovepipe went right straight up through the roof. And one day Sam had his tractor driven right up close and was filing the diesel tank so he just swung round and poured some of that diesel oil down the stovepipe. I guess he hitched the lock on the door first. Why, he said that stove fairly hopped right up and down. Finally, they got a window out and got outdoors. Another time, moving the shanty, Dusty Melindy, he worked for Flint a long time, he's gone too. But he was in the shanty and they were going to move it. Sam hooked the door, then he hooked on to the shanty with this cable that he pulled the logs with and that would pull up. They said he'd go along aways and he'd raise that front end up two or three feet and then drop it. Dusty was inside with stoves and canthooks and the stovepipe come down. I guess they had quite a collection before they got there. That Sam was quite a corker. (8:7-8)

Most of the time John worked at the Flints' mill in Barre. Almost all the lumber went to the stone sheds to crate the granite. For this John sawed softwood. "That gets monotonous after awhile. Just stand there and make half inch boards." (1:9) In the summertime, however, when the stone sheds and granite quarries would be doing their repair work they would want timbers. For this Flints kept oak logs and John would saw six inch boards "out of fairly good logs." (1:9)

The Flints also had a "portable" mill in Orange that John had originally helped set up with a man called Red Williams:

> One day... I was turning for my father and the boss came in—Ervin Clark, and he said, "Nate wants you to go up to the other mill. They're all ready to line it up and hitch the machinery and everything." So at noon I went up and we started hitching down things and getting it lined up and everything was there, the saw, motor, planer, edger. We got it hitched up and together and finally Red and I sawed a board—after awhile. (10:9)

Later Nate offered to give John a hundred dollars bonus if he would go up to Orange and saw:

> Well, that sounded pretty good then, you know, so I told him I would. So it was about a week before Christmas. He come in one day and handed me this envelope and said, "I didn't know but your wife would want to do some Christmas shopping." When I looked there was five $20 bills in the envelope which looked pretty good to me. I warn't floating in money then. In fact I never was. (1:15)

John sawed up in Orange for two or three years. "That was a good little mill." (10:7) There were about twenty men working there—eight or nine in the woods, and the rest at the mill:

> We...built a little barn up to the Orange mill to keep the horses cause when we'd saw up there they'd have the horses and this dray to pull the logs into the mill with. And then we had a little dam down to the brook with a big pump and a hose to wash the dirt off of the logs...In the barn it was two by four studding and the side of the horse stalls we boarded up with plank so they wouldn't kick the sides out of the barn. Well, down in this four inches, yellow hornets built a nest. And they'd had the horses in the woods and come back to put them in the barn and found the hornet's nest right off. Had the big hose there. I can't think of the old fellow who said, "I think what they need is water." So we turned on the pump and he put the hose to them. That didn't do much harm. Finally we decided the only way to do was make a torch on the end of a stick and so we got one of them and we got rid of most of them... And didn't set the barn a-fire. But some of us got stung. I got stung on my foot. That fire would burn the wings off but he crawled up my shoe—pecked me on the side of the ankle there. Most of us got stung once or twice. (10:9)

John always said he got along better with Nate than his brother Jake. "Nate you could argue with. He'd holler some and so would I. But Jake couldn't holler, cause he'd get to squeaking when he'd try to raise his voice. I've had him squeaking a few times." (1:15)

Despite Nate's temper he was kind. When John was in the hospital having his gall bladder removed with some forty gall stones in it, Nate sent down a big green order slip from the office with the words scrawled across it in red pencil, "Heard you'd opened the quarry. Here's a little something. Didn't know but what you might want some cigarettes or something" with a ten dollar bill pinned to it. (10:6) Another time John was in the hospital and Nate came down to see him:

> I laid there, tubes in my nose, bottle hung up side of the bed. Nate stopped right by the door. "By God, you don't look very good." was the first thing he said. He talked awhile and he said, "I noticed coming down the hall some of the folks have a TV in their room. Don't you want a TV?" "I don't care much about TV." "I'll leave some money here and when I go home you have them put a TV in here." When he went out he left a twenty dollar bill laying on the table beside my bed. (10:5)

As I heard John say so many times, "He was a pretty good old fellow. We had our moments you know. Did us both good." (1:15

The work was steady at Flints. In the old days it was six days a week. Then in the fifties in delayed response to the state's forty hour week, the mill began closing at noon on Saturday. There weren't many vacation days in between, other than Christmas, New Year's, Memorial Day and the Fourth of July. When the Tunbridge Fair was in the middle of the week, Nate used to give the men Wednesday off to go to it. Around Memorial Day the men used to stop to clean the boiler and do any necessary repair work. They would also stop again for three days or so during the first of deer season, again to clean the boiler and make major repairs. "The little steam engine that run the carriage would lock up once in awhile. Had two, so if something happened we'd take that out and put in another one." (8:9) That might take a half a day. Cleaning and repairing the boiler was a longer process:

[They'd] take the top off, get down in there and pound that scale off of it... You put stuff in the water to prevent scale on the inside. And it used to be kerosene and soda ash that they'd use.. which worked good. [It] would prevent the scale forming and the kerosene would keep the valves all greased. But some regulation of some kind won't let them use that any more. I don't know why. That was what we always used. ...We put one [bucket] of it into the boiler twice a day. One in the morning and one along toward night as I remember it.

They would scrape the sides with a file or sharp piece of iron. "Puttering job, kind of. Cold—not too bad in the summer but miserable in deer season." (8:10)

John was working in Orange when Flints had to move their main operation. When they had first built the mill in Barre the land had belonged to the railroad and the only restriction, as the mill was within city limits, was that it not work nights. The railroad eventually sold the land to the city. The Flint brothers had had an opportunity to buy it, but they felt the price was too high. Three or four years later, the city decided to build Spaulding High School there and Flints was given a year to move. They found a new location on top of a hill and replaced steam with electricity. "It's a good mill. I sawed there some." (1:18)

In the early '70s, Flints was sold to Renes and Sylvo Chaloux who changed the name to Ren-Cyl Lumber Company. John continued to work there a couple more years, but his health was not good and he began to think of retiring. When they modernized the operation in 1974 John decided his time had come. The boss of the operation asked him if he was interested in sawing, but John's answer was no. "I said what little hair I've got left is the wrong color to start on one of those rigs. It's a good mill and everything, but wants a young fellow to start." (11:15) He was intrigued by the change, but he loved what he knew. As John said, "It's all sit and go and you don't have to lift or anything. It goes down rollers and you steer it one way or another. It's fun to watch them. And now the sawyer even has buttons on this lever that he pushes." (11:15)

LATER YEARS

But John could not stay out of a sawmill and he soon found himself helping Bob Hoffman set up another portable mill in East Montpelier. Hoffman bought a stand of pine and brought the mill into the woods and set it up. "There were just three of us; Hoffman, myself and the man behind, that rolled the logs onto the carriage, the turner you call him." (2:14) John went on to explain:

> Didn't have any edger, had to edge it all on the board saw. Takes longer. Bring the board back, put it on the carriage. Then bring it back, turn it over and do it again. It isn't the speediest way to do it. (11:9) We'd saw three thousand some days which was pretty good for three men. They used to figure a thousand feet to a man, but they don't now. Got to be more than that now the way they do things. (2:14)

Bob Hoffman remembers those days with great warmth. "Nobody ever made any money, but we had a lot of fun." Any time there was a problem, John would go to tinkering. By that time he had spent his life working with the old style Lane sawmill and knew all its vagaries. And according to Bob there were many. John had told him about his old boss, Frank Hemingway, who used to stomp into the mill with a kind of hitch to his gait anytime the engine was acting up, and say, "Christ Jesus, what ails her now?" This became a byword at Hoffman's mill. At least once a day something would happen and John or Bob would invoke, "Christ Jesus, what ails her now?"

Although Hoffman's was the last mill John worked at, he would take on short temporary jobs—just to keep his hand in. He worked for the Fosters who still run a family sawmill in Walden. They not only saw boards but have a rig to make clapboards and shingles as well. "One of the girls turns for (her father), rolls the logs on the carriage and she saws when he isn't there. One of the boys saws." (9:18) John took his place for three weeks while he was in the hospital.

But mostly he tinkered in his shop, sharpening saws, making donut hooks, cribbage boards or whatever else he set his mind to. He made a batch of little round pieces of wood and printed "tuit" on them. He would laughingly give them away, saying "This is if you can get 'round to it.'" He made his items for sale, but he was generous, and a great number were given away. There would always be a great flurry of activity around Christmas time when he would go about working for Santa.

John was the last of the journeymen sawyers. He never was on the payroll of a big corporate mill. Instead he was respected for knowing his trade and could successfully go from job to job as the season and work dictated. The best testament is that he never lacked for work. Even after he retired he was still in demand.

Towards the end of his life John helped Bernie von Trapp set up a Lane sawmill in Waitsfield. As Bernie said, "he grandfathered me." Bernie would go pick John up and drive him to the mill. John oversaw the project, offering invaluable advice that only one with a lifetime experience in sawmills could provide. His eyes sparkled as he told me that he had sawed the first board to go through the mill. Bernie described how he had watched John as he sharpened a saw. With it came John's brand of teaching—something that is reminiscent of how he learned from his grandfather, "just keep the saw cutting" and his father's lesson on how to file a saw. As Bernie said, "He never came out with lots of direct information. It had to be a friendship." It was knowledge Bernie absorbed and retained—and, as he claimed, how he learned best.

As I've said, over the years John was not only my teacher but adviser and friend. If I was working on a project, he always knew someone I should see or had a suggestion as to what direction I might take. Anytime I had a question, I could usually get it answered by John. When I was putting together a Vermont folk art exhibition he told me about spruce gum books and different whittlings done by some of the men he had known in the logging camps. When I turned my attention to stone sculpting, he introduced me to Rock of Ages and led me through the Hope Cemetery. He was always someone I could count on for the information I needed.

One February day in 1987 a message reached me—second or third hand—that a woman had called to tell me that her father—someone I had interviewed had died, and that his service would be in Cabot on Wednesday. An ice cold foreboding gripped

John Lamberton, tasting some freshly made maple syrup, 1980.

me. I had interviewed a great number of people, but there was no one like John Lamberton. And certainly I associated him with Cabot. It couldn't be. I called a mutual friend who said she had heard nothing—that John had been in the hospital, but she thought he was home. I heaved a sigh of relief. Maybe it wasn't John. Still I wanted to put all my worries to rest. I decided to call the hospital—and my worst fears were realized. He had died of pneumonia that morning. I knew he was not in good health, that he had been in and out of the hospital, but I hadn't thought any of these stays were life threatening. At least I hadn't let myself dwell on that possibility.

Death slams the door hard. But even in death, it is always life one thinks about. I remembered back to that first day I met John, thought of our many jaunts, how he savored a joke and kept a book where he wrote down only the punch lines, his interest in the world around him—in people and their vagaries in coping with life's situations. There was his endless fascination with sawmills and the activities within them—those activities and happenings that he had made so alive for me. It was the people, "Gory, he was an awful good old fellow"—and a way of life that he had recreated for me. Jake "squeaking," Nate and his profanity, the humor and the understatement, the noise of the machinery, the whoof of the exploding boiler, the tinkering with the equipment and always the cutting saw.

Three years later—almost exactly to that February day, I found myself in Lower Cabot and was drawn to the cemetery. I hadn't been in the area since John's memorial service. This was familiar country from our many outings together. His grave was easy to find. There sat a white granite mill stone with John's name and dates on the left and Hazel's on the right. On either side of the center hole stood two trees—one a softwood spruce, the other a hardwood maple. Their granddaughter Suzanne Roberts, had designed the stone and under John's name she had drawn both a crosscut and circular saw, while under Hazel's she depicted a pair of crossed knitting needles and a ball of yarn.

I remembered back to a conversation John and I had had a couple of times. He had told me about an old mill stone in the river above his house. "Pa said he can remember going down to the grist mill and old Henry Dow would be there and have that out on the horses picking new grooves in it." (2:20) He told me he wanted to retrieve it for his cemetery stone. "Someday when I have a lot of money I'll go up and get it." That day had never come for John. But after his death his family set about finding the mill stone. Unfortunately they discovered that tons of debris from a garage had been dumped into the river over the stone and that there was no way to get at it. They put out the word that they were looking for a mill stone and a friend from Cabot called to tell them that there was one in the river up where his father lived. With a good deal of effort, this one was successfully removed. At first glance it was blue in color and coated in mud, but once it was

John and Hazel Lamberton's stone. Hazel died on July 12, 1993 and is buried with John.

cleaned and polished, a lovely white granite emerged. To the family's delight they discovered this was the mill stone from the first mill in Cabot.

As I stood there, on that cold bleak day, knee deep in snow, gazing at the stone I had to smile. It encompassed so well all those things John felt were the most important in this world—family, sense of place, history, the old ways and of course, the sawmill.

NOTES:

1. My thanks go to John Lamberton's wife Hazel, his brother Bob and his daughter Ginny for answering all my questions, making the photographs available and for reading different versions of the piece. I would also like to thank Bob Hoffman and Bernie Von Trapp for sharing their reminiscences of John.

2. All quotations are from taped interviews or fieldnotes. The first number refers to the number of the interview which is in the Vermont Folklife Center Archives, the second number gives the page number where it is located in the transcript.

3. A kitchen junket is a dance that would be given in someone's kitchen. The participants brought food, the kitchen was cleared of furniture and the fiddler often played sitting on the table.

4. The stickers allowed air to circulate through the lumber.

5. The horse supplies the power to operate the saw by walking the treadmill.

6. Gunpowder was believed to be an effective home remedy for sinusitis, a disease that is prevalent in chickens. Their sinus' swell up and they can't breathe.

7. A scoot is a single sled with heavy wooden or steel shod runners used for hauling logs.

8. That it was bad luck to begin anything on a Friday was a commonly held belief.

****

FIELD RESEARCH AS COLLABORATION: GETTING TO KNOW GEORGE DANIELS
by Gregory Sharrow

"I WAS RAISED BACK WHEN YOU LIVED ON A FARM AND DONE WHAT PEOPLE DO."

I first visited George Daniels on a rainy October afternoon in 1988. I was doing field research for a radio series about farm life and Bob Dumville long time Royalton resident had suggested that I get together with George. I had met George years before when I was working at a greenhouse in Randolph. He made balsam wreaths in quantity and I'd driven down to his Royalton greenhouse to pick up a van load. I'd recently noticed him at the Vermont Sugar House, a combination restaurant, gift shop, and tourist attraction near the Bethel exit off the interstate. I later learned that he worked there pressing apples in the fall and making syrup in the spring. When I saw him there he was on the prowl, looking for people to talk to, and I remember thinking he was their own "colorful-old-timer-in- residence."

I didn't know what to expect of George. I had a vague memory that he had been rather gruff with me when I came to get the wreaths and he didn't have much to say when I called to set up the interview—very few people do, though. I'd lived in Vermont for fifteen years, I'd always kept an ear out for history, and in recent years I'd done quite a bit of interviewing. I'd heard a great deal about what life had been like here in the past, especially in the era when most people had cattle and social life was centered in the neighborhood. In some ways these stories were very much like those I'd grown up with in Indiana but life here had its own peculiar flavor and there was much that was new and unfamiliar to me.

George ushered me into his trailer and set us up at a little table in his kitchen. He'd just gotten out of the hospital and I was concerned that the visit would be too much for him. He assured me that he was happy to have the company. He was all ready for me—he'd fished out a photo album and one of his grandfather's account books, and as soon as I'd set up the tape recorder he began showing me photographs. As we looked at these images he started telling me his story—the story of his life, the way of life of his youth, and his "disgust" with the ways of the modern world. I was looking for informants, people who knew a great deal about farm life past and present, and who could describe it well and in detail. George, as they say, was "my man". He was steeped in the traditional lifeways of Vermont, cared passionately about them, had a keen mind, lots of time, and loved to talk. We were off and running.

What George and I set about doing in a series of visits and interviews spread over the course of a year was to explore life in Royalton as he had known it in his teens and twenties, as well as the various experiences which comprised his life history. In the process we talked a great deal about attitudes and values which he attributed to an earlier way of life and his perspectives on the changes he'd witnessed in the ways Vermonters live.

"IF YOU NEVER HAD ANYTHING YOU DON'T MISS IT."

George Daniels was born April 11, 1910 on a hill farm a mile and a half above the village of Royalton. He was an only child. His Daniels grandparents had moved to Royalton from Rowley, Massachusetts, in 1901. According to George the Daniels family had lived in Massachusetts from time immemorial and his repertoire of stories included one about a Daniels ancestor who had deserted during the French and Indian War. His grandfather and great uncle had run a shop in Rowley that manufactured wagons. When the two of them decided to part company, his grandmother's doctor said she needed to get away from the coast and up into the hills. Another uncle had a farm for sale in Royalton and that's where they ended up.[1]

George told me much about his family's experience in Massachusetts, especially about the wagon shop and how it operated. Although he'd visited Rowley from time to time as a child he'd absorbed most of this information by listening to his grandfather talk about his life. That was one of George's hallmarks—he was interested in the past and what he heard stuck with him. His history included both his own experience and stories he'd heard others tell:

My grandfather worked on a marsh when he was a kid. Used to be all the marshes down to Rowley, marshes was all cut every year. My grandfather used to tell about when he was a kid his father and his three brothers used to go down—they'd leave at four o'clock in the morning, it was seven miles from where they lived to the marsh.

And of course they walked. He had to carry—everybody that was going to mow had to carry a scythe snath and two scythes, a gallon of water to a man, their meals, the hay poles, the rakes, and they had to get there when the tide was out.

As the tide was going out you followed it down mowing and then as it came back up you followed it back up. Then of course it was all raked by hand. Then they pile it up and stick a pole under each side of it and a man on each end pick it up and lug it to where they was going to stack it.

George's father was still a boy in 1901 when his parents came to Vermont and he went to school in Royalton village where he met and later married May Joy. May's father was a blacksmith in the village and had learned his trade in a lumber camp in Pittsfield known as Little Michigan. Again, George was heir to stories about the history of this branch of his family:

My mother's father was an unknown. He was bound out when he was three-four years old. That's all we know. Later years he discovered he had a half-sister somewhere. He came from Hubbardton. And he was bound out in Hubbardton somewhere.

That was when you had to start a business on your own. If you was bound out you worked till you was twenty-one, legal age. Whoever you was bound out to had to give you a pair of shoes, a pair of overalls and a shirt, and a ten dollar bill, and you was on your own. Way he put it, he headed right up over the mountain to Little Michigan and got a job up there in the lumber camp, and that was that.

His mother died and his father married again. It all happened very fast, I guess. She had children of her own and they started raising a family in the first six months. He was unwanted property.

This is the way I've always been told—that this guy come there and wanted, he had a pair of oxen he wanted to sell and they couldn't get together on a price, eight-ten dollars or something. The guy says, "If you bind the kid over to me until he's twenty-one, I'll give you your price." He says, "Sure, okay." And that was it. He just wanted to get rid of him anyway, and if he could get five bucks for him, why so much the better.

Now there's one other funny thing, too. My mother's grandmother, Grandma Parker, she died at our place. The only name that

I know of was Parker. Her son owned a store up there in Pittsfield. His name was Fred Morrill. In the town records he found she'd been married five times. And nobody living in our generation ever remembered her having a husband.

But she lived to be a hundred years old. She was a big woman, six foot tall, must of weighed two hundred pounds naked. She run the boarding house up there in Little Michigan. I don't know where she come from or any more about it than that.[2]

George went to the same school his father had attended in Royalton village. He talked at length about his school years but his memories of this experience were interspersed with a running commentary on what he remembered as an entirely different, and now vanished, way of life. Rather than simply describe what things had been like, George also wanted to make a point about the fundamental differences between now and then:

Talking about schools, they've changed since I went to school. I started school when I was eight years old, cause my folks thought a mile and a half was too far for a kid to walk. And of course you didn't have snow plows, you had rollers or horse teams.

So I started school in 1918 and walked back and forth a mile and a half, night and morning. Once in a while a girl that lived up where Hulls live, if it was storming to beat hang, why her grandfather would hitch up a horse and come down and I'd get a ride up far as there.

But it was very seldom that anybody got a ride anywhere. I mean, everybody worked back then. I can remember my father, when he was eighteen, nineteen years old, going over to the neighbors for some reason one day. And he went in the house and he said that the man and two of his sons was in there reading. It was a rainy day.

And it was the first time he ever saw an able-bodied man in the house in the daytime. He went home and told his folks. He couldn't understand why they was in. Because on a farm there's always something to do.

By George's telling, he didn't enjoy the Royalton village school, principally because he didn't like the teacher. He remembered her as harsh and unreasonable and claimed that he suffered undeserved penalties under her oppressive regime. School was held in a large building and heat was always an issue. During his first year snow would blow up through cracks in the floor:

127

Then in the next room they put a big furnace and up here next to the ceiling they put in about a thirty inch radiator. You can imagine how much heat you got sitting under there in a desk on the floor. The ink wells used to freeze all around.

So when it come—it got so cold nobody could do anything. So they had somebody come in and build some saw horses. I don't know, high enough so they could put planks across them. We could sit up where it was warm on top of the room. Wonder nobody ever fell off and broke their neck. Probably would today. I guess back then us hillbillies didn't feel like falling.

Then it come later on they decided to move us into the room where the furnace was. Well of course the furnace, you know how much heat you get off the sides of them. You don't get any. So they never could heat the place.

I think, what would the kids think today? That's the way it was.

When I got out of the fourth grade the teacher that taught in the next district started boarding at our place. So I shifted then, went over to the same school where she was teaching. We lived mile and a half either way. Wouldn't make any difference which way you went. Used to be three miles between schools. Nobody had to go over a mile and a half.

I think the smallest school I ever went to, I think the last year or two I went down here there was seven in the school. Eight grades, some grades didn't have any. And I think the most that was ever in a grade that I was in was, I don't know, couldn't ever been more than three or four. I know when I got out of the eighth grade there was two of us.

George went to high school in South Royalton for a year and then went up to Randolph Center where he enrolled in a two year program in agriculture. Ill health brought him home before he graduated and he went to work with his father on the farm. According to George he never regretted leaving school. He valued what he learned but felt that formal education was of limited utility:

As far as I'm concerned it never made a tinker's dam whether I had a diploma or not. Because you got all that knowledge stored away in here like you have in a computer, and if you want it and you get the right frame of mind, it comes back to you just as clear as can be.

They talk about high school educations, got to have them. But what good's a high school education if you aren't going any further, except that you can't get a job unless you got one?

But as far as a job's concerned, what difference does it make? What do they learn in high school that is necessary to do half the work in the country? My grandfather never went to school in his life but he learned to be a clapboard sawyer and a blacksmith. And when the autos come, he went from blacksmithing to mechanic in a garage in Barre.

Like other area farmers the Daniels family eventually made the transition from shipping butter to selling fluid milk, and with a herd of fifteen to twenty cows the cattle represented a significant portion of the farm operation. Times were tight during the depression and just as things should have been looking up disaster struck:

> ...my mother, my grandfather and my grandmother all died within eleven months. One of the neighbor's cattle got abortion,[3] they got into ours and we lost the whole herd of registered Jerseys, which at that time they paid you twenty-five dollars apiece. We had the '38 hurricane that blew millions of board feet bottom-side up and the price of logs dropped down out of sight. Most of it still lays right there cause you couldn't afford to take it out of the woods.
>
> And we lost our shirts, that's it. So we picked up our bag and baggage and moved off the farm. Federal Land Bank took that for fifteen hundred dollars, two hundred acre farm. But you couldn't hire money cause there weren't any. You start over again.[4]

George and his father moved into a lumber camp and their prospects for the future didn't look good. Within a year, however, their luck changed and a chance meeting unexpectedly brought a new beginning:

> Friend of mine came along one day, it was the winter and he had some beech logs to draw into a mill in Hartland. He said they're icy and slippery and it was stormy and he said, "You want to go down with me and help handle them?" I said sure, so we went down.
>
> Went down to Ernest Martin down to Hartland. And I'd never seen Ernest Martin in my life. We went down to his office and we was sitting there talking and Ernest says to Kenneth, he says, "You're getting married right off."
>
> Kenneth says "ya."
>
> He said, "Somebody told that an old farm up in Barnard got a lot of timber on it." He says, "Do you know anything about it?"
>
> Kenneth says, "No, I don't. Never heard of it."
>
> He says, "Well, if there's any timber on it," he says, "why don't we

look it over, and if there is, we'll buy it and if you get married you'll have a place to live."

Kenneth says, "I'm going into the army, I don't want to be tied up with an old house or anything else."

So he turned around to me and he said, "You know where it is?"

So I thought a minute and I said, "You mean the old Lockland place?"

Ernest said, "Ya, that sounds right." He said, "You know where it is?"

I said, "ya," I'd been through it years before the hurricane.

He says, "Why don't you go look at it?" He says, "If anything there's worth buying," he says, "call me up."

So the next morning I walked three miles up the hill. And I just went into the edge of the woods and I didn't dare to have anybody see me cause there was a knoll there covered with rock maple. They run five, eight-foot logs to a tree.

So I didn't want—if you see somebody looking at a lot—you don't want them to see you. Because then they'll figure there's something there and all hell breaks loose. If you go look at a lot you do it very secretly.

So I just backed right out of the woods and went over to the next house where there was a telephone and I called up Ernest and I says, "You be up here tomorrow morning and you bring up the money."

And he says, "How much?"

And I says, "Eight hundred dollars." And I says, "Don't want you bring a check, bring eight one hundred dollar bills."

Ernest says, "OK."

So I met him up there the next morning.

This is a fairy tale, I'm telling you. Cause there we are living in a lumber camp, no place to go. We was there just one winter, my father and I. Mother died back, I told you, during the depression, three of them died within eleven months. That's one of the things that sunk us, funeral expenses, doctor's bills and all that, cause there was no insurance back then. You were on your own.

But anyway, he come up and he went over there. And I says, "Ernest, all you want to do is just go and look in that one place, and then get out of here."

So we went over and I showed him just what I'd seen. Never went the other side of the road where most of it was. He turned around to me and he says, "What's this eight hundred dollar business?"

And I says, "That's what the guy told me he'd take for it. Cause I asked him."

So we went over to see him, he was an old Frenchman. Ernest got talking to him about hunting and fishing, got his mind off everything but his pocket book. After a while he says, "Well, you told Daniels here you'd take eight hundred dollars for that farm."

"Well," he said, "I've been thinking about it since then. I think I ought to get a thousand dollars. There's a hundred seventy acres of it."

Ernest said, "Well, that's OK, man's got a right to think whatever he wants to." But he took those eight one hundred dollar bills and laid them in a row right across the table, just like that. And we just set there and talked.

And after awhile Ernest says, "Well, you think you ought to get a thousand dollars?"

And he says, "I, I think so." He says, "It's a hundred seventy acres and they tell me there's some timber left on it."

And Ernest said, "Well that's OK." He reached down and started to pick them hundred dollar bills up and that guy grabbed them so fast he pretty near set the table on fire. I knew a check wouldn't look to him as big as eight one hundred dollar bills, cause the guy probably never saw a hundred dollar bill in his life.

So he says, "Go right down today and make the deal." So they took off.

Oh, Ernest turned around to me after he went out of the house and he says to me, "George," he says, "you don't know me and I don't know you. But I'm going to make you a proposition."

He says, "You and your father want to move up on that farm and log that, I will send the truck up and draw the logs, put 'em on the skidway front the house, and every thousand feet I'll give you ten dollars. Four dollars on the price of the farm, four dollars for the timber and that'll give you two dollars to live on and feed your horses."

And that's what we done.

When we'd cut a hundred thousand feet we owned what timber was left and we owned the farm.

George and his father's new home had lots of timber but little else. The ancient house needed a roof and had few amenities. It was seven miles up in the hills on a nearly deserted back road, too remote from the highway to ship milk. The fields were run down and viable cropland was in short supply. But George was happy to have a place to live and he and his father settled in to piece together a living on the old-time model:

Now I have always been, I try to always be self-sufficient. We went on that farm and everybody says there's no possible way you can do it. And when we went there, there was herds grass blossomed in the middle of the road. The only thing that ever went by there was the mailman. But within a year after we went everything picked up.

Greg: What year did you move up there?

Oh, forty-one, two, in there somewhere. Right after the

depression. We raised this and that and the other, I made wreaths, and I cut pulp and logs and wood, there was always something going.

One year everybody had pigs to sell and they weren't selling. And my father said any pig that you can buy for three dollars, we better buy it. And we bought a lot of 'em. Built a hog house and come deer season they weighed eighteen-twenty pounds apiece. And I'd dress off two or three and hang them up out front the house. And people going home from deer season come along and give you ten dollars apiece for them. Things like that, little things.

Then I built a cider mill and I made a pile of cider up there. Back then was when people used to use cider. I mean, one guy always had six-seven barrels, others have four or five. Practically every place put in at least one barrel of cider. And now they spend it for beer instead, that's all the difference there is.

Hard cider was standard drink. My mother said when she was a girl she never remembers sitting down to the table, weren't a pitcher of cider on the table. Never had tea or coffee, they had cider. Probably cost you five cents a gallon to have it made, it wan't very expensive.

Never sold hard cider. If anybody has measles and they don't break out, you give 'em hard cider and they'll break right out quick. So every little while there'd be somebody come along wanted half a gallon of hard cider cause somebody had the measles.

Well, evidently somebody, the great I ams, one day this fancy car drove in the yard, this guy got out of the car, I knew the son-of-a-gun was a government man the minute I see him. You could smell him, you know what I mean. You can. You just recognize 'em, that's all. He says, "I understand that you sell a little hard cider."

I said, "Never sold hard cider in my life, fellow." I said, "I sold a lot of vinegar."

"Well," he said, "that's what I mean. You sell me a gallon of vinegar?"

I said, "Yes, sir." I went down in the cellar and I drew him a gallon of vinegar three years old. Sold it to him for fifty cents.

He got in the car and drove down just around from the house. I snuck out where I could see him. He tipped it up, took one swallow of it, and swung that thing against the stone wall and I never saw him afterwards.

But we done about everything you could think of. We bought a new Leader evaporator, sugared up there. Put six-seven hundred buckets out. Oh, I don't know. There's always ways of making money if you want to go after it.

We used to buy calves. Well, we started in with some goats. And as soon as they begun to milk, we buy a calf and feed him goats' milk. And the calves grow like hang with it. They never have the scours or anything on goats' milk. So we raised them up and then bred 'em and

Four generations: George Daniels, his grandmother Eldora (Bray) Daniels, his great grandmother Mary (Scott) Bray, and his father Edward Daniels.

when they was ready to freshen we'd sell them, cause we never shipped milk.

Usually had a beef—bull we dress off in the fall for beef. Of course you always had your own vegetables, beef and chickens, eggs and pork, you didn't buy much. That's the trouble with farmers today. They take in so much money they don't raise anything, they buy everything. If most of 'em had spent a third of the time they spend on the road to home raising a garden it wouldn't cost them a third as much to eat.

I can't imagine anyone not having food in the house. Now I've got potatoes and beans and squashes that'll last me to spring. You won't starve to death—my father used to say if you got a quart of food for every day during the winter you never go hungry. May not be what you like but it's food.

George also had an apiary and kept his hives in a bee house, he ran a camp that catered to people from down country—his flier read "Your host, George A. Daniels, is in constant attendance"—he built a greenhouse and sold plants and vegetables, winters he rode the Barnard town plow, and for several years he cornered the local butternut market. During their years on the hill George and his father became a kind of local institution. They were gregarious and got around to see people. They had holiday meals with former Royalton neighbors Ray and Ida Hull, and friends would come up to stay with them, especially during hunting season. George managed the affairs of the household and did all the cooking. They lived comfortably without electricity—as George observed, "If you never had anything you don't miss it"—and some of the time they got along without an automobile—"When things got tough and you couldn't afford to have one I didn't have one."

George's life went along like this for nearly twenty years until his father's death in 1961. Shortly afterward he started making the seven mile trek to the Royalton store on his tractor to help storekeeper-postmistress, Mildred Davis, with the heavy work of lugging boxes and stocking shelves:

> Mildred and I was married when I was fifty-five. Her husband died about the same time as my father. After a few years Mildred and I got married and moved down here and have been here ever since. She was postmaster twenty-two years. And we had the store just twelve years after she and I were married.
>
> Greg: So you had a taste of store life then on top of everything else. What was that like?
>
> Oh it ain't like being out and breathing God's free air. But I had to be downstairs six o'clock in the morning. See, mail come in at five minutes to six in the morning. I'd get up and do the mail in the morning and go up and wake Mildred up and have breakfast.
>
> And then we'd come down and do up the mail. See, we had the Star Route that went from here to East Randolph. And the last mail didn't go out till six o'clock at night, so I was there from six to six.[5]

George and Mildred sold the store and Mildred retired as postmaster when the Royalton office was phased out in 1975. They set up a trailer on a long strip of land between the village and the river; George built a small greenhouse out front and had several acres of garden in back. At the time of Mildred's death they'd been married nineteen years.

In the meantime George had sold his land in Barnard. He told me once that he was credited with having "ruined" that area of the town.[6] George's strong feelings about his rights as a property owner gave rise to his outrage at legislative attempts to control development. His comments underscore the very real and widespread tensions between traditional attitudes toward land ownership and statewide initiatives to control growth. Always a canny operator, George managed to get as much as possible for every acre of land he sold:

> I sold everything on the hill piecemeal along. This is something that amazes people. After my father passed away I was there alone. He and I of course lived alone for twenty odd years. But different friends from down country wanted to buy places to build camps.
>
> And I told three real estate agents that I would like to sell some of that up there and I wanted one hundred dollars an acre. Well, you ought to hear the ha-ha-ing of anybody paying one hundred dollars for an acre of land. Wasn't nobody would pay that for an acre of land up here. So I never sold a piece of land through a real estate agent.
>
> But I did sell a lot to different people. And the way I sold it—a lot of Polish boys came from Connecticut and so forth. And they'd buy an acre of land for a hundred dollars and give me ten dollars. And when they paid me a hundred dollars, I gave them the deed. That's just the way it was, all written on a piece of paper and a receipt.
>
> Of course Act 250's killed any use of having property anymore, cause you don't own your property anymore. I think that is the most illegal thing they ever done. And that's why my folks left England was account of the crown owning property. You didn't own anything in England, you rented it from the crown. The last piece of property I had sold for five thousand dollars an acre.

When I started visiting George his health had begun to fail and he'd been forced to give up many activities that he enjoyed. Dizziness had prompted him to quit driving and he no longer took produce to the farmers' market in Randolph. He'd had to scale down his garden and this past summer he hadn't had the stamina to do much work in it. He'd phased out his greenhouse business and only made a few wreaths each Christmas as special orders. He hadn't given up entirely, though—his garden was still large by most people's standards and he kept the greenhouse heated throughout the winter. He felt that death was near and he was biding his time. In his words, "You just got to wait for it to come."

George had a stroke in 1989 just after Thanksgiving. He was hospitalized for a week but regained his strength quickly and was able to return home and continue living alone. His step-daughter lived next door and was in and out regularly to make sure everything was going well. I had talked with George on the phone and had arranged a visit to discuss this essay—George said he was anxious to see me because there were some things he'd been thinking about that he wanted to tell me. On the morning of the day we'd planned to get together the local funeral director called to tell me that George had passed away suddenly the day before—January 14, 1990.

"IN THE SUMMERTIME EVERYBODY USED TO HAVE SWIZZLE."

George took it upon himself to teach me the lifeways of the world he had known as a young man. And I of course was eager to learn. A knowledge of plants, both domestic and wild, was an interest we shared in common and was one of several strong threads of connection which ultimately bound us together. We compared notes on the progress of our gardens, discussed the cultural requirements of particular plants, and I quizzed him about gardening in the past. As always his supply of information was seemingly inexhaustible and his knowledge and interest were part of an on-going family tradition:

I had my first garden when I was eight years old. There was a woman on television one night telling about the old Green Mountain Guard, got started back in the first World War. Well, I belonged to it and that's how I had my first garden.

My grandfather had a garden, always, a big garden; lived out of the garden. On the farm you didn't buy nothing, you never had any money to buy anything with, wan't nothing you needed.

Two different years we had a cottage on Plum Island off Newburyport. You know I couldn't wait, course you went back and forth on the train. When we come home, I couldn't wait to go and look at every pumpkin, watermelon, corn stalk and everything there, cause I was always so interested and I missed it so like hang—that week.

See my father was very interested in the outdoors. He liked to hunt, he liked to fish, he liked to log, he liked to grow crops, he liked to be out where you could have animals.

And I'm the same. I'd be lost if I didn't have some dirt out here to play in, 'cause that's my recreation. How much harder is it to go and hoe a row of potatoes than it is to go down and throw a baseball for two hours when it's a hundred degrees?

Of course when I was a kid every farm kid hunted ginseng—the whole family. My father started taking me in the woods when I was probably four years old. Get home from church Sunday, have dinner, and if there was a good afternoon he'd take me in the woods and tell me different trees and plants and shrubs and all this stuff.

And I got where I knew pretty near every living thing in the woods. My mind isn't good enough now to remember them all.

You know there's something that's funny now. Kids never get out of the village. They never think of going back in the woods for a walk.

137

When I was kid and when my mother was a girl, same thing, pick up and have a lunch and go back in the woods for a mile and have a picnic together. And go up some cave somewhere back in the woods.

You can't get a kid up there, they're scared to death. Bears and elephants and kangaroos!

Paralleling George's interest in plants and the natural environment was his life-long involvement with music. Again, music was part of his heritage from his family, and, again, his memories offered an opportunity for me to learn much about the fabric of daily life in the past:

Music is something I love. My mother played the piano, my father played a coronet. My grandfather played a violin. On the other side of the house, my grandfather didn't play but his father played a violin, played a cello. My grandmother on my father's side played the piano, organ. There's music in the house all the time.

My great grandfather used to play around for weddings and funerals, he played cello mostly. I've got the cello. When I found it it was in my second cousin's up in the bedroom. Found it over in a corner with a bunch of junk. I knew what it was in a second.

My mother said that I was four years old when I picked out a first tune on a piano. My father gave me a violin when I was sixteen years old and I wouldn't go to bed that night till I picked out a tune on it. That's how I learned, I guess.

George was well known locally as a fiddler and played regularly with a group for public dances:

Lee Hull's wife, Sally, and Lee, Russ Olmstead, Buddy Benoit, used to be different ones in and out. We was the ones that played most of the time, played down in Sharon for years down to the Grange Hall.

Greg: Was it all kinds of music? Or square?

Mostly square, square and round. Didn't have this modern stuff then. When they first come out with it Buddy Benoit was into it head-over-heels. He used to play the guitar. But he didn't play—I liked Buddy's playing because he played the melody.

Now all they do is scrub. I mean all they do is have a rhythm, they don't have any tune. But Bud would play just like you'd play on a violin or a piano or anything else, he knew what he was playing.

And he told Sally, he says, "If we're going to keep on playing you got to learn this new method."

138

Well Sally says, she taught music for many years, and she says, "You bring me the sheet music and I'll play it."

"Oh," he says, "you don't have sheet music, you go ahead and make it up as you go."

Well Sally said, "Would I waste my time trying to play something that doesn't have tune enough so they can put it on a piece of paper, I'm not going to waste my time trying to learn to do it."

And that was the end of that.

For a number of years kitchen junkets were also a part of George's musical milieu and he played for dances around his neighborhood:

Three or four different places there you'd have them. You didn't want more than fifteen-twenty people there, weren't that much room, all square dancing. Sally played the piano and she'd just bring us in.

She used to say we was the only orchestra in the state that always played, never had a rehearsal—cause we never played together except we played for a dance.

Greg: When did kitchen dances die out?

I'd say in the thirties probably. We had to quit just because it got where you couldn't have one because every gall darn—always some joker was there with booze. You get somebody with a bottle on their hip and they don't have kitchen junkets.

Like one night, having one right up here in that big square house on the hill. They had a Round Oak stove sitting in the room there, stovepipe all off it, some joker threw a match in it. It was full of papers.

Always seemed though something happened. Somebody would get a friend of theirs that come in bring a bottle, next thing you know they'd smashed the window out. It just got where you just couldn't have them anymore.

People now got to raise hell, they can't have a good time just doing something, you know.

George had a piano in his living room and on my first visit he sat and played for me. He produced a wild storm of sound with a strong melody line rising out of a whirlwind of related notes. He emphasized that he played for his own pleasure and that he had no formal training in music:

I can't play so you'd probably recognize what I played but I get a lot of fun out of doing it. I don't know much anything about notes or time or anything.

It's an odd thing; I don't know how you'd explain it. You play the piano? The funny thing is it don't make any difference if you got your eyes shut or not. Right? You don't have any control over your hands, do you?

Your brain controls your hands but if I'm playing something and I stop I've no more idea where that next note is than the man in the moon, most of the time. Let me show what I mean. Good practice for an old man to keep his fingers limber.

I think that probably any tune I ever heard, if I were in the right place at the right time, I could play it. It'll be all stored in your memory, sometimes it'll come out, sometimes it won't, but they're there.

Every time I hear the tune that I just played, in fact the one before, I smell coffee. Because when they come up for a coffee break, we always played that and it gives the kitchen notice you're breaking for coffee. And I still smell coffee every time I play it.

Greg: I'm amazed that you can work out two hands for these.

It's just like learning to eat, I guess. You learn to use a shovel and then you learn to use a fork.

George once told me that when he and his father lost their farm they took only their clothing and a piano with them when they moved to the lumber camp. Now as an older man with failing health the scope of George's world had shrunk and his piano had become all the more important:

This living alone, it's a lot of entertainment. Lots of times I get ready to go to bed at night and I walk by the piano and set down and play for half an hour. It's just a way to pass the time. My cats, my pipe and my piano, that's my family.

As with so many other things, George Daniels was also a repository of information about the foodways of an earlier way of life. As tastes in food had changed he had never adapted; he still cooked and ate as his parents and grandparents had at the turn of the century. He told me once about an old neighbor of his who was equally set in his ways:

This modern diet wouldn't agree with him. He used to boil a kettle of potatoes every morning, fry two strips of bacon, two strips of salt pork, and when the potatoes was done—he'd cook enough to last him all day, make three meals.

Set 'em in the sink and run cold water over them till they was cold, cut 'em up in chunks and then pour the grease from the ham bacon over them and stir them up in the frying pan and have that about three times a day.

He got bad we had to take him up to the hospital and he had a fit. Went up there and they charged him all this money and he couldn't get a decent meal. By gosh, he got home the first thing he done got his frying pan out fried up some salt pork because he felt weak. He'd lived for seventy odd years and that's what he'd lived on.

I even now don't feel like I had a meal without a potato. We always had warmed-up potatoes for breakfast. Course then you went out and you'd work two hours before breakfast. And you went in the woods and swung an axe six-seven hours, when you come home to supper you wanted something beside a cream puff and a gob of nothing. And you always had potatoes.

On one occasion a conversation about food held an unexpected surprise:

My grandmother on my mother's side, Joy, she said she never remembers having tea or coffee on the table, but they always had a pitcher of hard cider and everybody drank it. And she never remembers seeing anybody drunk. They used it like the Italians use wine.

And in the summertime everybody used to have swizzle, right. It's vinegar, maple syrup, and molasses and a little ginger. But they used to figure it was better for you than 'twas drinking so much water. Haying everyone had a jug of swizzle.

And there was a piece in some paper and Cliff Brooks was talking about it the other day. So he was talking along here and I went over and I didn't say anything. I made some and handed him a glass of it. And he said, "That's the first time I've had a glass of that," he said, "I bet for forty odd years."

Greg: Oh. What's this?

Don't ask questions.

Greg: Oh. Okay. Ummm.

Swizzle.

Greg: This is swizzle? Wow, it's great.

I suppose, as Cliff said, if you put that up half a cup in a bottle and sold it for fifty cents you'd make a fortune.

Greg: Now it's water, maple syrup, vinegar and ginger?

That's it. Years ago if you didn't have maple syrup you used molasses. Same thing. But it quenches your thirst better than water and I guess the ginger probably is good for you in hot weather. I don't know, farmers used to say so.

George and I discussed preserving food:

You didn't have any refrigeration so you smoked your ham and bacon and hung it up in the cellar. It kept quite awhile hung up in the cellar, got a good smoke on it. Now you can't even buy a smoked ham or bacon.

Greg: Your folks cured your own meat at home? Did you soak it in brine?

It takes the same pickle for ham, bacon and corn beef. Bacon you leave in about four weeks and ham six. We used to have barrels. In the cellar you had a barrel of salt pork. You always had your cider barrels and your potato bins and your apple bins, canned stuff, beets, carrots, turnips, cabbages, you had all that stuff.

Greg: And after it soaks—

Hang it up in the smokehouse. Should be smoked three or four days. Depends on how warm it is. We had a pit way down in the ground, a can in the bottom. Built in four feet square on top of it. Hang your meat in there and throw a few coals down on the bottom and a handful of corncobs.

And of course where no air's getting to it it just sits there and smolders, makes smoke. The more smoke you get on it the longer it'll keep. Probably wouldn't touch it if it's got a lot of smoke on it. We used to smoke hams and shoulders and hocks and bacon.

There is a few local smokehouses, I guess, where they do have cob-smoked ham. Most of it's just painted on with a chemical. And they inject brine into the joints.

Greg: And when you salt greens—

Put a layer of salt in the bottom of an earthen jar, put a layer of greens and throw in some more salt. Just about like making sauerkraut. Just leave it. Had a weight on it so you could keep it under brine. But make its own brine, of course.

You want it you fish it out and let it sit overnight in fresh water and freshen it out enough so you wouldn't take the the skin off your mouth. Be kind of salty. But that was all there was to it.

Greg: What kind of greens did you salt?

Now you probably never ate many of them. Dandelions, milkweeds, narrow leaf turnip tops, cowslips, beet tops and turnip tops, red rooted pig weed—butter weed we used to call it. Rich, beautiful tasting, way ahead of spinach or anything like that.

Years ago people used to do things to make things keep. My great grandmother died at our place. She was a hundred years old when she died. She couldn't cook anything without either rum or boiled cider. Cakes, pies, anything. Had to have one or the other.

We also talked about menus and the ubiquitous role of salt pork:

Greg: As a kid what was a staple for you family food-wise?

Potatoes, beans, pork and beef in the wintertime.

Greg: What about breakfast? What would a breakfast consist of?

Hasty pudding, sometimes fried pone, ham and bacon, eggs, warmed up potatoes with onions, I mean real food.

My father, the time we had boarders in 1918, he got on to corn flakes and he ate corn flakes for years for breakfast. He always wanted something to go with them cause there's not much to a corn flake unless you put some potatoes and meat under it.

I was up store one day back when present owners bought it, Vicki was waiting on me, I wanted a piece of salt pork. She brought a slab out, I said give me half of it. The girl stood there and says, "Can I ask you a question?"

I said, "Ya, ask me anything you want. If I know, I'll tell you. If I don't I'll shut up."

She says, "What in the world do you do with salt pork?"

I said, "I eat it."

She says, "How?"

"Well," I said, "you use it in baked beans, you use it in pork stew, you use it when you dry apples, you make pork gravy out of it, you can fry it or boil it or eat it raw."

She stuck up her nose and walked out and I think she thought I was the biggest liar that ever lived.

Now my grandfather—and I know a guy up on the hill used to do the same—he loved to make a pork sandwich. Get out your pork barrel, fish a piece of pork up, cut a slice off about half an inch thick, put it between two pieces of bread and eat it.

Salt pork sandwiches weren't George's only suggestion—he was a veritable compendium of salt pork recipes and he was ready to describe these to me in complete detail:

Another thing—I haven't seen anybody besides myself ever had fried apples anymore.

Take salt pork, cut up in giblets like your little finger, throw it in the frying pan, let it get so it's brown, a lot of grease in there. Just slice up sour apples, sour apples are better than any other kind.

Cut them up in chunks and throw them in there, put a cover on, keep stirring 'em up and that pork grease and the pork itself mixes in with the apples. Oh my gosh is that good. People don't cook much anymore, you know.

Greg: What's a pork stew?

Made out of salt pork. Just potatoes and milk. Onions. You fry up your pork like you would for fried apples, little squares, till it gets nice and brown, I like it so it's little crispy. Slice your potatoes and onions up and put 'em on the water like you would anything else.

When they're done, you dump the water out, dump that pork fat in, and cover it, put milk, salt and pepper and a little butter in, heat it up hot. Gosh darn good. I love it.

There's an awful lot of food we was raised on that people never heard of anymore. I can't imagine how some of these fancy restaurants, they call Indian Pudding a gourmet food.

Indian Pudding was something that if you're so poor you couldn't have anything else, anybody had a bucket of cornmeal and you could make Indian Pudding.

Nothing to it. What's it take? Two tablespoons full of cornmeal, quart of milk, something like that. Very, very little of anything but milk in it. If you had raisins or something to throw in, so much the better.

For George contemporary foods didn't hold a candle to his old favorites. It wasn't so much that the old foods were intrinsically better—although he might have argued that they were heartier—but the old foods were what suited his tastes:

My daughter over here, step-daughter, she's always sending me over something for supper at night or something. I don't want to hurt her feelings but I'd a hell of a lot rather have a boiled potato and milk gravy on it, you know.

She's great for spaghetti—and then they use a oregano and sweet basil which to me are the most horrible smelling and tasting things in the world. Oh Christmas, no! I use salt and pepper.

"IF YOU COULD PICTURE THIS COUNTRY LIKE IT WAS... "

George Daniels was an accomplished historian. The history he kept was every bit as rigorous and carefully crafted as that of any professional, but his research techniques, topics of inquiry, and modes of presentation clearly distinguished him as the practitioner of a specific genre. In the parlance of folklore studies he was a folk historian par excellence and the love of history came naturally to him.

George's interests were wide-ranging. He once took me on a car tour of his former haunts and we visited mill sites, stone chambers, foundation holes, farmsteads, and fence rows. He told me a story about almost everything we saw and the stories ranged widely over the past two hundred years. As he pointed out the ways in which a barn had been successively enlarged or a farmhouse altered, he drew not only on his own memories but on the collective memories of generations past. He was always very precise about what he did and didn't know—when I asked a question he couldn't answer he said so.

As a young boy George spent lots of time with older people. He and his parents lived with his Daniels grandparents and as George observed, "My grandfather was the one that taught you. My grandfather was old enough so he had time to talk to you where your father was always working more or less."

George's grandfather wasn't the only older person in his life. The neighboring farm was owned by the Wild family and the patriarch of that household, old Deacon Wild, was also a person George knew well:

> ...he was a minister, he lived to be ninety odd years old. So he was an old man when I was a kid. So his history went back quite a ways. I spent a lot of time with him.[7]

Deacon Wild told George stories about his youth but George's heritage from this man was more than stories—his name never came up without some mention of shaving shingles. George's memory was a repository not only of history but of special skills and work routines. Although he no longer had the tools to shave shingles George had the know-how and this too was something he was eager to share:

> The biggest part of shaving shingles is to find a tree that you can make shingles of. They always made 'em out of hemlock--of course you never cut a hemlock for shingles unless it was two foot on the stump or something. You try to find a tree where the limbs come out and hang down on a hemlock. Because they will—straight grain, split easy.
>
> You see, with a crooked grain your shingles are cockeyed. I've cut spruce that was that big around and the limbs hung down and it split just as smooth as a sheet of paper.
>
> Greg: Why if the limbs hang down is the grain going to be straight?

George Daniels peddling his plants and produce at the Randolph Farmers' Market. George always had a big garden and in later years became an institution at the Farmers' Market.

I have no idea, but that is the way you do it!

Greg: You cut hemlock two feet—

Ya, then you saw them up in blocks sixteen inches long or whatever length the shingle. And then you halve them and quarter them. And then you start on the edge and split the shingles off.

Well then, you got a thin shingle same thickness on both ends. Thin as you can. Then you just put them in a horse and shave one side down, turn it over and shave the other side down.

Then take a little off each side on the thin end so that when you lay them down you got a little space on the end there so they wouldn't lap over or something, fit better if you just take a little bit of the edge off.

Greg: Did most people make their own shingles?

No, back when I was a kid, this old Deacon Wild—he died before the first world war, he was an old, old man. Back then if you got old and probably the shape I'm in, they'd have a sawhorse and a place out the barn, spare room in the house where you set there and shave shingles. I mean that was one of the things they done to kill time. But you see hand-shaved shingles would outlast sawed shingles two to one. And people say, why? Well, you stop and think why. Use your head.

146

Greg: Well, let's see. Hand shaved, if it's hand shaved there wouldn't be any tooth marks in it. It'll be smooth.

It'll be smooth, right. And straight grain so the water runs off, where a sawed can be any old way. Cause if it isn't straight grain you can't split it for shingles, right? If it isn't straight grain you get crooked shingles.

During George's youth there had been an outbuilding on his grandparent's farm which years before had been used as a hop house. He described this structure to me in great detail—it's been rebuilt now as an apartment—and he told me bits and pieces of information he'd heard and observed about life on this farm in the past:

They claim that during the depression after the Civil War, there where Peter lives, that they killed a hundred and fifty sheep and buried them out there. Well, they saved the hides and tried out the tallow and fed a lot of the carcasses to the hogs, because they wasn't worth anything.

And when the hogs was grown they killed them and buried them the same place they did the sheep cause they couldn't get a dollar apiece for them. And they claim that on that piece where Peter is that at one time they sold fifteen hundred dollars worth of hops one year, which in them days was a lot of money.

According to what the guys used to tell me—you see a hop vine comes up from the ground every year. So when they get ready to harvest the hops they just cut the vine off at the ground and pull the pole out. And they put them under cover and the girls and women around the neighborhood would come in and pick the hops off.

And then they'd spread them apparently upstairs in this building here to dry. And there was an open shed under that and there was a place where they could hang a bag—and apparently they shoveled them down through the floor into a bag.

But there was up this side—just adjoining our place up here—there was a hop yard, but when they put the interstate in they buried it twenty feet deep. The hops are gone but you see there was a mound every check row and those mounds was there like little ant hills, about an acre in there.

And when I was a kid there was hops growing all around the edge of the fields and so on. But this was hop country. And then—according to what the old timers told me, it went from here to California and that's what killed this hop business down here.

Another thing is, what was all open land and pasture, two

hundred years ago was all maple. And that was all cut and burned for charcoal. Every little while when you're plowing, you'd run into a charcoal ring in the ground, big circle fifty foot across and charcoal mixed in to the soil.

And they cut all that maple and burned it for charcoal for blacksmiths shops. The evidence was there when I was a kid. According to what these old-timers used to say that was all big maple years ago. It was two hundred years ago probably.

George spoke as witness to the unique events of his lifetime. The log drives in the White River were going strong during his childhood and he talked at length about such occupationally specific topics as booming the river at Sharon and building flush dams in Rochester. I especially enjoyed those memories which clearly reflected a boy's point of view:

When I was a kid that was one of the great attractions in the spring, waiting to see the first log come down the river. When it come across the bridge over here everybody was in a hurry to see.

They filled the river with logs as soon as the ice went out. And then as soon as they got all done dumping them in there'd probably be seventy-five—a hundred men, bateaux, and they had teams along on the river bank, followed them, cook wagon and all that stuff, tent. And they come down and swept the river—everything went ahead of them.

They used to eat their lunch—there used to be a covered bridge over here--and they always had boiled eggs for lunch. After the log drive went through there'd be a streak of egg shells along the timbers all the way across the bridge where they set there eating eggs, 'cause they fed them four times a day.

'Cause they was in ice water up to their neck all day. And nobody ever took their clothes off, of course, you'd lay down and they cover you with horse blankets and you steam dry during the night. That way nobody catches cold.

When I was a kid, if I got wet my mother would no more of thought of letting me change my clothes because if they dry on you you won't catch cold. Cause see, she was born in a lumber camp up in Little Michigan, up above Pittsfield, four miles back up in the woods.

George not only talked about how things used to be but also described how they evolved. He interpreted change for me and detailed the evolutionary process by which the past was transformed into the present. His grandfather had been a

148

blacksmith and as George explained,

Blacksmiths turned into garages. It's hard for people to think that now. That's how my grandfather, when he quit running the blacksmith shop and sold it, went to work in a garage. That's where the mechanics were, in blacksmith shops.

Greg: So they just learned a new trade then?

That's right, like you learn a new style of horse shoe or a different way of bending an iron. Cars weren't too complicated when all they had to do was go up and down the road you know.

George acted as custodian for all manner of arcane historical data. He told me once that he had quite a discussion with his wife about the word "stook", a term he used to describe bundles of corn left standing in the field. His wife called them shocks and to quote George, "I used to say, you'd have to be pretty good to shock a pile of corn up into a stook." George also told me stories about the legendary Joe Peavey who designed the lumberman's tool that bears his name and about the origin of the term clapboard. This information was courtesy of his blacksmith grandfather who had worked as a clapboard sawyer up in Little Michigan:

Of course a clapboard, what we call a clapboard actually is a clear board. That is what it's supposed to be but it's like a lot of things, you shorten into something simpler.

Greg: What's it supposed to be?

It's actually supposed to mean clear board—no knots. And of course it's quarter sawed so it lasts forever. But you never used to see a knot of any kind in a clapboard. Then they got so they changed the name and changed the quality the same time, I guess. Clear board was a clear spruce board, there was nothing else.

George's talk about the past was ethnographic in the sense that it was vividly descriptive but he also wanted to make a point. For George commentary and description went hand-in-hand. History didn't just sit there—it had something to say:

Saturday night's the night you took a bath, changed your clothes for Sunday morning for clean clothes. It'd last you a week. Bathtub in the middle of the kitchen floor.

If you're lucky enough, if there weren't too many of you, you had warm water enough. If you didn't, ya froze to death. But you took a bath whether it was warm or cold. Everybody took baths Saturday nights. That was standard procedure.

You had two pair of overalls and two work shirts and two frocks. You stripped off the ones you wore on the week before, they went in the wash tub Monday, what you put on would last you that week.

When I went to school I never knew a kid that didn't go to school Monday morning with clean clothes and wear them the whole week. Never changed them, didn't have anything to change in. Nobody had eight pairs of pants and ten coats.

You know—that's another thing. Everybody had a cobbler's box, cobbler's hammer and awls and shoe pegs and wax thread and bees wax. If you got a loose sole you didn't go and throw your shoes away, you either cut your own out of a piece of hide or went to the store and bought a sole and tapped it on yourself.

Now you can't do that because shoes are made out of this stuff that you can't nail to. You can't drive a nail into this plastic stuff. Back then shoes were all leather. You could sew it and you could stitch it. And you mention Neat's Foot Oil today and most people look at you like they don't know what a neat and an oil is.

That's what makes shoes last.

This one here's got a crack on this side. Now if you get a little hole like that, you throw the shoe away. I don't know what the hang difference it makes: if you got a hole on top to put your foot in what difference does it make if you got a hole on the side to let the air in! One thing is money comes so easy. Throw it away!

People today have too much, it all comes too easily, they don't appreciate what they have, they don't know what they want—these were all themes that came up time and again as George talked about the world of his youth. These themes were stated outright and each formed a core around which a particular story was organized. But others of his stories were more like fables with an unstated moral embedded in the anecdote. It was up to me to draw my own conclusions:

Back in 1939 we bought the Porter lot. It had been logged sixty years before. One of the guys that was cutting it back sixty years ago, he was a neighbor to us. Well back then he broke his leg up there in the woods. And this guy come up to get a load of logs—old George Smith, he was laying alongside the road. He said, "What's wrong Mister Smith?"

150

"Broke my leg."

"Oh," he said, "I'll get you right on the sled and get you down."

He said, "Put your damn logs on, don't go down empty. No sense going down just cause I got a popped leg."

So they put a load of logs on, piled him on top, and took off.

As an old man George felt cut off from the mainstream, marginalized by a whole new way of life. The things he knew and valued were relics in the modern world and his history bore witness to another way of life:

> It seems to me that there's an awful lot of information just dying of my generation's. It's probably all, as I always say, non-essential stupid knowledge.
>
> It's a changed world and I've outlived it. Let's face it. You know. Things I'm interested in nobody else is.
>
> But if you could picture this country like it was when I was in my teens and twenties, you wouldn't ever believe that it could be like it is now.

"...WE HAVEN'T GOT BRAINS ENOUGH TO LEAVE THINGS ALONE."

George Daniels the historian cannot be separated from George Daniels the social critic. In order to understand his history it's essential to also understand what he valued most about life in the past. We must ask what George saw as the most significant characteristics of the world of his youth and how he related that experience to our situation in the present. Some might dismiss George as a sentimental old man who was preoccupied with nostalgia for his lost youth. That was undoubtedly true in part but there was also much of substance to what he had to say.

In many ways George's history-making parallels the thinking of such folklorists as Henry Glassie who insist that scholarship offer alternatives with power to challenge the present. Drawing on the past to critique contemporary life is not at all unusual. Environmental activists, for example, refer back to the balanced relationship traditional cultures maintained with the natural environment as an exemplary model against which to measure current practice. Their celebration of this relationship is motivated by a strongly felt need in the present rather than nostalgia for a perfect past.

George questioned the fundamental assumptions on which contemporary life is based. From his perspective the old way of life was more rational, humane, environmentally sound, and held a greater potential for personal satisfaction. George was convinced that life in the present had gone awry and that civilization, so-called, was moving in the wrong direction:

> You look around the world and you see every place in what we call civilization has been introduced is the end of that country. And we haven't got brains enough to leave things alone. Look what we've done to the Eskimos.
>
> Look at the people in Peru. Those places people lived there for thousands of years, the same way they always lived, they're perfectly happy, perfectly contented. And why do we have to go in and destroy everybody's way of life.
>
> Indians had a way of life and they never destroyed anything, did they? They harvested what game they wanted to eat, but they didn't go out and shoot it just for the fun of shooting it. They might shoot each other some but so do we.
>
> I think people are going to self-destruct in time.

When George reminisced about the world of his youth he concurrently railed at everything that was wrong with the present. Occasionally his critique seemed far-fetched and I came close to dismissing it as nonsense. But his comments were never arbitrary and were always grounded in common sense and his own remembered experience:

> Course it's hard for me to understand why kids now all bring homework home with them. Because when I was in school you could've brought it home and you could lug it back but when are you going to do it? I mean, that to me is such a change that kids don't have nothing to do.
>
> ...they had to build a—buy buses to carry the kids to school. And they had to go in debt to do it. Then they went seventy-five thousand dollars in debt building a gymnasium so they'd have a place to give the kids exercise because they didn't get the walking. So it's a losing proposition all the way around.

Confronted with the non-logic of contemporary life George

consistently looked back to what he considered to be a saner world. From that frame of reference such pressing current issues as solid waste management didn't make any sense:

> When I was a kid they didn't have any waste.
>
> Greg: Didn't you have any trash at all? When something broke or—
>
> You fixed it. When we lived up where Peter lives, every spring my grandfather would take the oxen and tip cart and pick up what accumulated during the year. Mostly about all he ever had was tin cans from when you bought can goods.
>
> Hell, we'd only have two bushel—in a year. Anything that would burn went in the stove and we had a little washout and we used to dump it off in there—tin cans and bottles and medicine bottles and that kind of stuff.

George emphasized the fact that the way of life of his youth was as an integrated system, and, like the traditional culture of the Native Americans, it worked well. People led full, satisfying lives, they had what they needed and no more, the resources they depended upon were renewable, and their lifeways were in harmony with the natural environment. I commented once that George had knowledge that was priceless, to which he replied:

> You have knowledge that I never heard of. Because you're probably a technician. Everybody is today. Everybody knows one thing, two things. Isn't that true?
>
> You know, one thing that always has bugged me and you hear it all the time on television. They tell about businessmen and farmers. Did you ever know a farmer that could be a success unless he was a businessman? And have you ever known a businessman that could of run a farm?
>
> No.
>
> Because they don't have the general knowledge. And if you're a successful farmer you got to know how to be a carpenter, you got to be a mechanic, you got to be a veterinarian, you got to be a butcher, you got to be all things.
>
> Right? Agriculturalist, you got to understand agronomy, you got all these things that—if I said something about agronomy to my grandchildren they'd think what the heck is that, what part of an airplane does that go on?

A major theme in George's critique of contemporary life was the observation that today everyone is a specialist, a technician. From George's point of view people today have only one thing they know how to do and they depend on other people for everything else. On my first visit I asked him if his family's farm had primarily been a dairy operation and I was somewhat taken aback by his answer:

> It wasn't primarily—never believed in having it be primary anything. Of course we had cattle, we had sheep, we had hogs, cut logs, we sugared, we raised crops to sell, I mean it was just a farm.
>
> Today there's no farms left. They're all dairymen; I don't call a dairyman a farmer. They don't raise nothing except a field of corn and some hay. Go out and buy their vegetables and buy everything. They don't farm.
>
> Years ago milk and eggs was the wive's money. You done the milking, brought the milk in the house and she could make whatever she wanted; make butter, cheese, but that was her income.
>
> But you didn't figure what you got out of your cows had anything to do with money on the farm. You got your money out of farming. Logs, wood, bark, potatoes, chickens, pigs, there's always something you could scrape up for money.

A sense of the fragmentation and compartmentalization of modern life was at the root of much of what George had to say. When he railed at the specialist he was reacting to a paradigm of contemporary social organization. The logic of managerial bureaucracy and industrial mass production is deeply embedded in our thinking about how the world works. George, however, grew up in a world modeled on an entirely different system and he consistently referred back to the values of that system:

> An awful lot of farmers, of course, were half-blacksmiths. My father wouldn't think of hiring a blacksmith to shoe a horse no more than my grandfather would hire a wheelwright to build a wheel; he built it himself. He might have to go buy a new tire for a farm wagon. But you take it home and set it yourself.
>
> My grandfather had a cider barrel that had a bad stave in it. He just take it all to pieces, take the stave out of another old barrel and put it back together. He could fill it up with cider or water or anything.
>
> Any one of them things that years ago people knew how to do. I hate to see anybody today take a barrel apart and try to put it back

together. Especially if they had to substitute pieces. But with a spoke shave if it was too thick or too wide you could shave 'em make 'em fit.

My grandfather of course was a wagon builder and a carpenter. We had a wagon wheel break when he was on the farm. He whittled out the spokes, got the fellers sawed out on the band saw.

Greg: What would get sawed out on the band saw?

The fellers. The outside rim of a wooden wheel. Then he'd build a fire and heat the tire up and set the tire. That was a hundred dollar job have a wheel rebuilt. Nothing to it if you know what you're doing.

George's grandfather's experience as a wagon builder was of course a special circumstance but George's point still stands: when he was growing up people who lived in the country were independent and could do many different kinds of things for themselves:

I think that people back then, I won't say they were more intelligent—maybe it was a case of necessity. But they was more self-sufficient. They knew what they wanted, they didn't ask somebody else to do it or hire somebody to do it.

Everybody knew how to butcher a hog, take care of the meat, build a house or raise a crop of stuff or alter a hog or anything else. Good Lord now, you raise a litter of pigs, they go and hire a veterinary to alter the pigs and it costs as much as the pigs' worth.

My father had a jackknife, must of altered 10,000. He used to have it done—make a little slit, took the ball out and filled it up with fine salt. Pig wiggle his ass a little like that and go trotting off and that's the last you ever heard of it.

Farms as George remembers them were relatively self-sufficient enterprises. They were small, there were lots of them, they gave people a living, and they were an integral part of a system which from his perspective supported a superior way of life:

You take a farm where there's been a couple lived on it and raised two or three kids, put them through graded school and if they was girls they usually, some of them went to high school.

But they ate, they was fed, there was clothes, they learned life as it was then. They was capable of going out into the world and making their own families and not bother anybody.

That's gone.

As quoted above, George maintained that there are no farmers left in Vermont, only dairymen; from George's point of view this was symptomatic of the transformation of the whole of rural life. Obviously the trend toward specialization was the product of a complex series of interrelated forces and there are many possible ways of interpreting how this came about. George's version gave voice to the perspective of people who were, in effect, its victims and his comments represented the old-time farmers' point of view:

Ernest Martin told me that his grandfather lived in the town of Barnard, that would be a hundred and fifty, two hundred years ago. He was a darn good farmer, raised everything—you grew your own clothes, you raised your crops, and you had your taxes and maybe two or three dollars a year, you had no use for money.

As times changed and you had to have money he lost his farm because he couldn't change because he was used to farming the way he always farmed.

If you went up over the hill here, there's place after place where they raised big families. A lot of them had two or three pair of horses and they'd send them into logging woods in Rochester, Pittsfield, Hancock, winters drawing logs, and they could make enough to come home and not be in debt.

But when they went to selling milk, there wasn't any roads to collect milk. Like when we first shifted from making butter and sending it to Boston, we used to separate the cream and they sent a guy around collected the cream once a week it was, maybe twice a week or something.

But if you lived back up on Johnson Hill or somewhere, they didn't go up there because there was no way of getting there. The roads weren't good enough so they could—

And then of course when trucks come that screwed the whole thing up again. A lot of the farms

George Daniels (center), with his father Edward (left) and Grandfather Moses Augustus.

156

used to cut logs and take 'em to the mill in East Bethel or South Royalton or the Bethel Mills up here.

Well then they started plowing the main roads but they didn't plow the back roads. So you couldn't take a load of logs and go to the mill unless you had a wagon half way down to change from one to the other. That cut off income a lot.

Now I had a friend up in Barnard, neighbor, he was a veteran first world war and they was French family, he was an old batch, lived there with his mother, and he used to milk about twenty cows, always had full-blooded Jerseys, nice ones. And raised three, four acres of potatoes. And they had a darn good living.

And he come over one night, used to come over to the house a lot, "Don't know what the reason is," he said, "always had plenty of money. But some reason," he says, "seem to always be spending more than I'm taking in."

Well that was the whole key—when you got where your taxes, instead of thirty dollars was three hundred, when your fire insurance that used to be twelve dollars was ninety-eight, you had a pickup on the road instead of a driving horse, you know, you bought your grain instead of raising it, you had to have a tractor—those are the things that killed farming.

"PROBABLY IT'S US OLD COOTS THAT ARE WRONG."

George Daniels linked past and present in an on-going dialectic. His memories of the past called forth all that he found missing in the present and the problems he saw in the present suggested the better world of the past. His critique of the present had a number of major and related themes. By bringing these themes together here we can clearly see what he thought was wrong with contemporary life and his design for a better world. One theme predictably had to do with money:

People have to have things now that when I was a kid, the king never heard of it or couldn't afford it if he had. But now money don't mean much. It's so easy to get and easy to go.

The first money I ever earned was right up here in this store before it burned. And during the noon recess—we had an hour off at noon I used to go up there and put groceries on the shelves. And he used to give me my choice of three cents or a chocolate. And I never took the chocolate, I always took the three cents.

There's too much money around. Too easy.

When I was on earth I could cut a cord of wood in three hours and a half and I got a dollar and a half a cord. That don't figure out too much an hour. Done it all with an axe. Now it's hard to find an axe you can cut a chicken's head off with, they're all so damned dull.

A parallel theme had to do with the role of work in daily life and the ethic of staying busy:

I never woke up in my life in the morning but what I had something to do. And I can't understand people saying they get bored, they ain't got nothing to do. Guess there's enough to do you go out and look for it. I can't imagine the time that people just waste.

They don't seem to have any imagination to find work anymore. My mother, of course we had a big family of us and never saw a washing machine until the last few years. Never had electricity, get water for the tea kettle in the reservoir on the stove.

But she had time to make hundreds—she used to knit booties, some company they used to send her the yarn and ribbons and everything. That and baby jackets. She used to make piles of them in her spare time. Where now they sit and watch television.

My grandmother and my great grandmother made hooked rugs. They made braided rugs, my mother used to make hooked rugs. I cut my foot one time and I was about two months I couldn't step on it. And I made three hooked rugs while I was sitting in the house.

We would do something like that rather than just piss away the time.

**Haying on the Daniels' farm, when "every hand had to do."
Moses and Eldora Daniels pitching on (center), George
Daniels treading down (right).**

George's comments on industry applied not only to adults but also to children:

> I was up to the doctor's yesterday. And I said something about how it looked to me that they was growing a whole generation of fat, flab, too much food and too little exercise. And he agreed with me.
>
> If you got up in the morning and milked three-four cows and walked a mile and a half to school and got out at four o'clock and walked a mile and a half home and went out in the pasture and hunted up the cows and got them in and done chores again, you didn't have to have much sports for exercise, you know.
>
> Kids now will call up and want you to take them, they're going two houses home, you got to get in the car to take them. Something wrong somewhere. Probably it's us old coots that are wrong.

George questioned the value of education as it had evolved in the contemporary world:

> Is there a limit to education? Let's say that they pass a law now that every kid is entitled to a college education. What are you going to do with them? Can they buy paper enough in Canada so everybody in the United States can set on their ass in an office building and write? Or punch computers?
>
> Do you ever stop to think, how many college educated people do anything for good of the world? Do they produce anything necessary for life? Just think about it.
>
> You think about it. You know probably five hundred college graduates. Well, what do they produce except paper?
>
> Greg: People do all kinds of different things, you know.
>
> Well name one thing that they do necessary for life.
>
> Greg: It seems like doctors are fairly useful.
>
> Doctors are.
>
> Greg: Teachers—
>
> Teachers aren't cause they don't teach anything. I mean the teachers today are as ignorant as the kids were when I was in school. We had a better education when we got out of the eighth grade in school than they have now out of the high school.
>
> I think that a lot of their learning, they put too much emphasis on things that don't amount to a tinker's gosh darn.
>
> I bet you take the average kid out of the seventh or eighth grade, give them a pocket full of matches and a hatchet and drop them up there in the woods somewhere—they probably wouldn't know enough to get supper. And it's all right there in front of you. But I guess that's the way the world is today.

Another of his themes had to do with pace and its impact on family life:

> The whole world to me—probably crazy, I know I am, of course, hear it every day—but people are too hyper and everything's moving too fast.
>
> The music, the cars, the—they advertised a new one here on this car show the other day, the only car made with a speedometer that goes up to a hundred ninety miles an hour. But where in tarnation do they, where do they use a car that run a hundred and ninety miles an hour?
>
> I think people are too pepped up, I guess the lifestyle that does it, but Lord, they're not at home, they got to go somewhere all the time.
>
> Used to be families worked together. Now everybody gets up in the morning, they take off like a bunch of pigeons in every direction. Night after night you look over at my daughter's, both cars are gone, house all dark, everybody's gone.
>
> Homes aren't like they were. I tell Kay she hates her home, she hates to stay in it. If you liked your home you'd stay in it. But they don't anymore. It's just a place to change your clothes and go somewhere.

For George, as for many older Vermonters, community life was a charged topic and the changes during his lifetime stood out in sharp relief:

> There's no community anymore as far as I'm concerned. There's no neighbors. How long since you've been to one of your neighbors and played cards at night or something like that? You don't! Everybody's gone. Busy doing something or watching TV.
>
> Greg: Were there entertainments in the summer, community entertainments?
>
> Oh, ya, all the time. I mean there ain't any entertainment anymore. Church socials and card parties and dances and, oh, Lord, I don't know. And cracker and milk socials. Now these kids would think it was crazy.

Finally, George repeatedly commented on the shift which had occurred during his lifetime from the everyday use of natural materials to the use of synthetic materials. For George this change summed up a host of related changes in lifeways of rural Vermonters. In the world of his youth George's neighbors had raised crops and animals; today many commute to factory or service jobs in Hanover, White River, or Lebanon. An agricultural society has, in effect, been drawn into the mainstream of our national industrial and technological culture. And from George's perspective these changes were mirrored in the things that people use:

>I like life better than I do death. Now everything is dead. There's no life in that microphone, it's some old rancid oil come out of some prehistoric rotten fish, when you get down to basics.
>
>I always liked to see anything grow. I don't care if it's a tree, a kitten or a jackass; I like life.
>
>Which today is a dirty word, right? Everything's artificial. Everything's artificial. Well, that pipe's artificial. You can't even buy a cob pipe with a reed stem anymore cause the only place they made them was out in Missouri and they gone out of business.
>
>What do you learn in school about anything that is living? Now it's all plastic, it's oil, it's metal. You go out some morning when it's twenty below zero, you put your hand on a piece of steel. It'll burn.
>
>All right. You put your hand on a hemlock board. Does it feel the same? The board's got life in it. It isn't cold.
>
>Years ago you lived on life, not death. Today you live on death.

"AIN'T TOO MANY THINGS I HAVEN'T DONE, EXCEPT MAKE ANY MONEY."

George Daniels was an inexhaustible source of information about daily life in rural Vermont in the past. He was the archetypal key informant, an extraordinary person who was thoroughly a part of local life but was also unusual—a "one of a kind," as people are want to say. He was uniquely able to reflect on and distill his experience into vivid language. In the process he spoke not only for himself but for his generation and his locale.[8] As I once said to him:

>George, you're an absolute encyclopedia!
>
>I ain't either. I was just raised back when you lived on a farm and done what people do.
>
>There's a lot of education living in the country that you don't have to pay for—if you keep your eyes open and have to live that way.

From my point of view as a folklorist, George was a great discovery. But folklore field work is uniquely personal and I could never separate our personal relationship from our professional one. It was research that brought me to George but it was more than

161

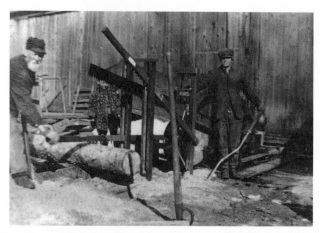

Cutting firewood to length with a drag saw rig. George Daniels (center) with his grandfather, Moses Daniels (left) and his father Edward Daniels.

research that kept me coming back. At first I remember feeling a responsibility to stay in touch. I brought him some of my pickles at Christmas and I'd stop in for a visit whenever I was in the neighborhood. But later I realized that George and I shared strong connections on a deeper level. Our mutual interest in plants, for example, was limitless. But more importantly, we both were folklorists. It was my unwavering interest in the history of everyday life that led me to become a professional folklorist and wander the countryside talking to people about their experiences; it was this same interest that made George such a powerful commentator on cultural change and the way things used to be. One of George's refrains was that no one was interested in the things *he* was interested in—to which I could reply, "I am."

Thus we were co-conspirators and every taped interview gave us both a great deal of pleasure. By the time I met him I had already spoken with a good many people about rural life in the past. It wasn't so much that what George was telling me was new—although much was—but that his description was vivid, rich in detail, and complete. George was personally introducing me to the world of his youth as he remembered it and I was completely engrossed.

There was also much that we didn't share. I was from the alien universe of doctoral degrees and people who write for a living and I don't think George ever had any idea what my job was. For my part I was often impatient with his inability to consider my point of view—there was no opportunity for me to be myself or talk about my life—and the relentless intensity of our interaction wore me out. I couldn't relax and visit quietly with George because whenever I was with him I was "on". Thus from my perspective our relationship wasn't easy. But in the end what we shared far outweighed our differences and our friendship worked well.

Several months before George died he had told a newspaper columnist that I was writing his life history. At the time the comment surprised me but now I realize that that's essentially what I'm doing. Several weeks after his funeral I visited his step-daughter to borrow photos. She was cleaning out his trailer and gave me his great grandfather's cello. Thus I became custodian of one of George's principal artifacts and have come to think of myself as having a kind of custodial role for his knowledge about the past as well. This essay is my attempt to create a portrait of George and share something of what I learned from him.

George and I recorded approximately eighteen hours of interview time. The material we covered ranged from topical commentary (including sociability, family life, work routines and the like), to detailed accounts of such specific activities as peeling hemlock bark, lining bees, and making wagon wheels. We recorded a great deal of information about working in the woods, the pulp and lumber market, logging camps, and the sawmill industry, as well as a series of coon hunting stories and a building-by-building tour of the South Royalton business block (circa 1920). These were all personal reminiscences in which George offered his perspectives on all of these things. In some instances his commentary took the form of a detailed description that left little room for interpretation; on other occasions he painted his picture with a broad brush and I can't help wondering if he stretched the facts to make a more compelling story. One thing is certain; however, the substance of what George had to say rings true. I've heard similar accounts time and time again; George's commentary represents a common pattern in talk about past life by older Vermonters.[9]

163

George offered an idealized vision of life in the past but it was nevertheless good history. He was skeptical of the notion of progress and concerned that the world was changing in ways that carried more liabilities than benefits. He mined the past for ammunition to deal with the present, and his conception of that past was shaped in the present. The world of his youth was gone. He recreated it to the best of his ability using the resources available to him. His vision of history was shaped by his purposes and world view. That's true of all historians and is, after all, what the writing of history is all about.[10]

In a sense George was also chronicling the emergence of post modern American culture. The Reformation, the rise of capitalism, and the beginnings of the Industrial Revolution set a social revolution in motion which is ongoing and continues to shape our lives.[11] The small-scale, rural, and familial society of 17th century English open-field villages so ably described by Peter Laslett in *The World We Have Lost,* fell victim to this revolution and represents a system of social organization which we have shed by degrees, during the intervening centuries. This shift from a model predicated on the needs of the group to one centered on the individual is at the root of what George and many others are talking about when they rail at the contemporary debasement and fragmentation of community life. Whether or not life in the past was indeed any better than the present is beside the point. The era of neighborhood work bees, of kitchen junkets, and of holiday "exercises" at the district school is unquestionably over. The fact of its passing and of its contrast with succeeding forms of social organization is part of the lesson we learn from George.

George Daniels enjoying his corncob pipe.

Finally, where do I fit in all of this? Every interview is of course the product of a collaboration, if you will, a jointly authored text.[12] I had an impact on what George had to say if for no reason other than the fact that I was there. I did ask questions, but not very many because once George started talking he followed his own course. The things that he told me were not spontaneous creations but ideas he apparently had already worked out in previous tellings. From visit to visit he sometimes repeated himself and although no two stories were identical word-for-word, many were nevertheless substantially the same. It's my impression that my interviews with George were shaped more by his agenda than by mine.

This essay, however, represents a substantially different process. As I mentioned above I had planned to visit George to talk through this project and invite his participation. I could see that it would add a new dimension to our relationship and I was sure that it would give him a great deal of pleasure. I had no idea how we would work together, but I was game to see what would happen. His death put an abrupt end to my plans for collaboration and left me with the responsibility of deciding what was important to George and what he really meant. I've spent many hours working with his interviews—selecting, arranging, editing, and contextualizing what George said—and I've tried to do it honestly and thoughtfully, keeping in mind that I wanted him to have the opportunity to speak for himself.[13] I find that with George's death my image of him has subtly changed. I can see that I tend to remember the best things about him and that he's gradually become a bit larger than life. I recognize that the George Daniels I've written about is an abstraction, a hybrid creation that ultimately represents and speaks for both of us. Thus my relationship with George has continued to evolve through the act of writing and the creation of the persona of this text.

NOTES:

1. The Daniels' family history is documented in a letter written by Etta Kinnear circa 1961 and a note written by George Whitefield Daniels circa 1855. Copies of both documents are on deposit at the Vermont Folklife Center Archive.

2. Charlotte Parker died in Royalton on Nov. 29, 1920 at the age of 88 (Deaths, book 13-22:223). Her husband's name was listed as Pliny Palmer. From vital records, Royalton Town Clerk's Office, South Royalton, Vermont.

3. "Abortion" is a colloquial term for brucellosis, a disease of cattle which causes them to abort. The brucellosis bacterium can also be transmitted through milk to people and the human disease is known as undulant fever. Brucellosis was common in Vermont during the early part of the century and infected herds were required to be destroyed.

4. George's grandmother, Mary Eldora Daniels, died May 26, 1938 (Deaths, Book 33-45:139); his grandfather, Moses Augustus Daniels, died Feb. 7, 1939 (Deaths Book 33-45:150); and his mother, Della May Daniels, died March 20, 1939 (Deaths, Book 33-45:152). From vital records, Royalton Town Clerk's Office, South Royalton, Vermont.

5. George's father, Edward Augustus Daniels, died Oct. 19, 1961 (Deaths, Book 59-68:317), and George and Mildred Davis were married Jan. 23, 1965 (Marriages, Book 59-68:337). From vital records, Royalton Town Clerk's Office, South Royalton, Vermont.

6. Hope Nash wrote, "The beaver pond over Barnard line where George Daniels and his father, of Royalton, had gone to live was still a novelty when George, unable to pay his taxes, about 1950 got permission from the town of Barnard to sell off small lots. He put up a sign by the beaver dam near the road: "Stop. See my beavers. Free picnic ground." He sold small lots on all sides, many of them to local people, and up sprang a village of shacks, A-frames, trailers, and all kinds of camps and small cottages. So the beavers were indirectly responsible for an early showing of what may happen to any pleasant country road, on no notice at all. From Hope Nash, *Royalton Vermont* (Royalton: South Royalton Woman's Club and Royalton Historical Society, 1975): 105.

7. Members of the Wild family were prominent in Royalton life. Their progenitor, Elisha Wild, moved to Royalton from Fairlee in 1833. Elisha's son, Deacon John Wild, lived on the home farm and was the old man George knew as a boy. His son, the Rev. John Wild was credited with having "probably the longest record for church membership of any one now living in town" (1911). He was elected deacon in 1878 and served as superintendent of the Sunday School for many years. He was born June 11, 1824 and died July 22, 1917 (Deaths, Book 13-22:122). From Evelyn Wood Lovejoy, *History of Royalton, Vermont with Family Genealogies* 1769-1911 (Burlington, VT: Free Press Printing Co., 1911): 1030-1033 and vital records, Royalton Town Clerk's Office, South Royalton, Vermont.

8. On key informant see Henry Glassie, *Passing the Time in Balleymenone: Culture and History of an Ulster Community* (Philadelphia: University of Pennsylvania Press, 1982), 13-19; on key text and the process of ethnography see pages 640-647.

WEAVING THE FABRIC OF OUR LIVES: COLLECTING ORAL HISTORY FROM FAMILY MEMBERS
by Rebecca Morse

INTRODUCTION

When I begin teaching oral history interviewing techniques to my students I tell them to avoid interviewing family members. No sooner are the words out of my mouth than a student says, "But the reason I'm taking this course is to learn how I can collect stories from the older family members before they die and the stories are lost forever!" A point well taken. Family members are important resources in oral history work and the importance of their knowledge is undisputed.

We begin to concern ourselves, then, with some very special considerations as we work through interviewing family members. Issues become personal and profound. Lives and stories are connected in ways we do not understand clearly. The interview

(Left to right) Rebecca Morse, Elizabeth Morse, Dorothy Rogers, 1990.

situation is steeped in emotion and risk for both the interviewer and interviewee. What emerges from the experience of collecting oral history from family members is a personal history within which the interviewer begins to understand the content of the fibers which make up his or her own life. Just as those of us who have grown up in a Judeo-Christian tradition can gain meaning and insight through the study of biblical narrative in an historical perspective, so family members can gain meaning and insight as they make connections to traditions, events and persons known to them only through the narrative traditions of their family members.

The interviewing I have done for this article has been emotionally draining. I have been uncomfortable. What began as a small project has grown; it is hard to know when to stop. It is more difficult still to sit down and sift through the thoughts which have plagued my mind through the months of this writing. How does one objectively represent the life story upon which interviews are based when so much is clouded by experiences and events in the interviewer's life and by the day to day interactions with family members as they have lived out their lives in a fabric often torn with discord? One doesn't. It is impossible to be objective; what one can do is look at the threads which hold these very different lives together and allow the power of the life story to impact on the lives of those who take the risk of knowing and attempting to understand the connections. A colorful and vibrant fabric emerges. I am grateful for the opportunity to interview my grandmother and mother and to facilitate the writing of my grandmother's life story. I am a different person as a result of this experience.

MY GRANDMOTHER, DOROTHY ROGERS

I first began interviewing my grandmother, Dorothy Poulen Rogers, in 1976. As a graduate student in folk studies and oral history, I was interested in collecting some of her stories of faith healing. She had spent several years of her life working and ministering in nursing homes around central Vermont, and I wanted to record the stories I remembered her telling me about that time of her life. I realized that faith healing was as much an option in Vermont as it was in South Carolina, Georgia and Kentucky. As I studied folk preaching in the American South, I wanted to compare

168

my experiences in rural churches in North Carolina, Tennessee, and Kentucky with the stories my grandmother told me about Vermont. It was during 1979 and 1980 that I interviewed my grandmother on the subject of preaching. I also accompanied her on some of her nursing home visits in Montpelier and Barre.

The last interviews were conducted during 1989 and 1990 in preparation for developing the framework for Dorothy Rogers' life history. All of the interviews prior to 1989 were done during visits to Vermont from my places of residence in Kentucky and North Carolina; however, I returned to live in Vermont for two and one-half years from 1988-1990. During that time I completed the interviews for this article. For me as researcher and writer, that return is significant as it forced me to focus on little known elements of my family history and to frame my life in the context of the Rogers family. Up until that time I had avoided any personal involvement with my grandmother's story. Living in Vermont for a time and allowing the elements of these interviews to distill, allowed me to come to terms with a portion of my history which was unknown to me earlier. The writing of this article has been a process of becoming for me.

As Dorothy Rogers' life unfolds within these pages, other voices speak to expand and color her own words. I found it valuable to interview my mother, Elizabeth Rogers Morse, to provide a generational link in the story. Her words add a special texture to the fabric. As granddaughter, daughter and writer of this article, I will at times add my own thoughts and memories to the story. Woven by using my grandmother's life story as the warp and those of my mother's and myself as the weft, the result emerges as a fabric, the texture of which connects the lives of three generations of Vermont women.

EARLY LIFE OF DOROTHY ROGERS

Dorothy Poulen Rogers was born on March 11, 1910, in the same house in which she now lives on Trow Hill in Barre, Vermont. The house was built by her great-grandfather, Chester Beckley. She explains:

The house has always been in the family. I hope it's always going to be. Right on the wall here is a picture of Grandpa Beckley and Grandma Beckley, the ones that built this place. And that was a good many years ago. My mother would have been 99 this coming December; this house was built quite a few years before that. (Aug. 29, 1989)

Chester Beckley, an immigrant from England, and his wife, Amanda Bassett, a Scottish immigrant, bought the land on Trow Hill from John Trow and began to clear it. They settled there on the hill, built the house now owned by Dorothy Rogers, and raised at least four children there.

Dorothy's grandmother, Lillian Beckley, married Hubbard Samuel Meaker and they had eight children. The oldest child, Ivis, died in the house at fifteen years of age. Dorothy's mother, Beatrice, was the third of the eight children. She acquired the house in her adult life and her children were born in the house. The house was passed down through the women of the family, a fact which I find particularly intriguing.

The house itself holds many memories for Dorothy. One of her earliest memories of the house involves the wake for her great-grandmother, Amanda Beckley. "I was about five years old. [She] laid in a casket right here. My brother, John [Chester], was only two years old at that time. He tried to hand Gram a pair of shears while she was in her casket there." (August 29, 1989) The wake lasted about three days.

Dorothy remembers her great-grandmother as a religious person. "She was Methodist. . . .and she had Sunday School classes right here in this room where we're taping. She was a woman who had received the baptism of the Holy Spirit." (August 29, 1989) Dorothy's grandmother, Lillian Beckley Meaker, was also a religious person, but she kept her religion yo herself. She had a Bible and "she had worn it out from reading it. She covered it over with some kind of cloth. And she never talked about the Bible to us." (August 29, 1989)

Dorothy remembers one Christmas when she and her Aunt Avis decided to hang up stockings for Santa Claus to fill. There was no fireplace, so they decided to hang their stockings behind the kitchen stove. "Grammy Meaker says, 'It won't do you any good.' And we thought, sure it would, we'd get something in those stockings, but when we got up the next morning, there wasn't a thing in those stockings. I'll never forget that; that has stayed with me all through these years." (August 29, 1989)

At age 16 Lillian married a man ten years older than herself:

My grandmother, she had to get married and maybe my Grandmother Beckley kind of looked down her nose on that. When anything like that happened they were always looked down on. And maybe my grandmother was looked down on by her mother, I don't know. ... And then my mother had to get married and my grandmother never liked me. (August 29, 1989)

Dorothy was the oldest child and felt much resentment. "They didn't talk about it but it was there. My grandmother died without even speaking to me; at the time she died she wasn't speaking to me." (August 29, 1989)

Lillian's daughter Beatrice was undoubtedly born in the house on Trow Hill. She married Raymond Poulen and had six children: Dorothy, Chester, Isabelle, Lester, Harold, and Tylea. Raymond was of French descent and a blacksmith by trade. He worked well when he worked, but "he was a drunkard." (August 29, 1989)

He'd go away and stay sometimes for two weeks. He'd take what they'd saved and he'd be gone. Use every bit of it. Like they would own a horse and they'd own a wagon and they would own a harness; he'd have a good suit of clothes. When he'd come back he'd come back with a pair of sneakers and a pair of overalls. That's all he would have. (August 29, 1989)

Because Raymond was away much of the time and could not be counted on for family support, Dorothy's mother, Beatrice, would work in whatever ways she could to support the family. The children worked too:

In the spring of the year mother dug dandelion greens and sold them for a dollar a bushel. My mother dug horseradish—this place was loaded with it—and she'd scrape that--we'd have to go out and help—great big nice roots, and she'd scrape that and have a great big pan of that all washed nice and clean. Put the food chopper out on the edge of the porch and us kids would have to grind the food chopper and she'd feed it that horseradish. You couldn't stand it in the house because you'd do some crying. She got sixty cents a quart for horseradish back in those days. Us kids would go and peddle it. Peddled dandelions, too. Used to have a big raspberry patch up here in the field. She'd go up and pick raspberries in that hot sun. And we had blackberries here, and she'd pick them. (August 29, 1989)

Beatrice took in washings as well. "She would wash on the washboard Monday and Tuesday. Wednesday and Thursday she mangled[1] the clothes and ironed with a hand iron." (August 29, 1989)

For years she didn't have electricity in this house and when she didn't have electricity she had to heat her flat irons on the stove. She didn't have a mangle for a long, long time so she'd take all us kids up with her to Grammy Meaker's to do her mangling. And there would be great baskets of clothes—sheets and table cloths and pillow   cases, towels—everything went through because she was a good worker. Shirts and everything used to look just perfect.

Friday she'd go down and do housecleaning downstreet.

Beatrice Meaker Poulen, (Dorothy Roger's mother).

Saturday we'd go out into this woods when there was no snow on the ground and we would throw wood--she with us--over the fence onto this side of the fence. Frank Trow owned the woods over there and he said we could have all the wood we could find on the ground. And that would all come over here onto this side. I can still see my mother out there in that barn with the old fashioned sawhorse with a buck saw sawing up wood to keep this family together when my father was off like that. (August 29, 1989)

The children were kept home from school on many occasions to work. Dorothy's Aunt Eleanor was kept home every Monday and Tuesday to help with the laundry. Her task was to turn the wringer on the washing machine. She also helped Grandpa Meaker do slaughtering:

Eleanor was a big strapping girl and she had to stay home and help do slaughtering. One day Grammy Meaker was down there helping. [They] cut the throat of the hog and the hog jumped up (you throw them on the back) and started to take off and run right between Grammy Meaker's legs. She was short-legged just like a squaw and she took off with the hog! There were some times you'd get some good laughs. (August 29, 1989)

When I was sixteen years old my little sister [Tylea] was born. And, of course, [my father] had left home when she was a month and a half along. He'd been gone for quite some time and Grammy Meaker knew that my mother was pregnant. We were up here in the garden just above the house and mother looked down the road here and says, "Here he comes now."

And Grammy Meaker says to my mother, "Bea, under the circumstances you'd better take him back."

I says, "If she takes him back, I'm leaving," because he had tried to get wise with me and I was not going to be around where he was. So she didn't take him back. (August 29, 1989)

Raymond died of pneumonia a few months after that; he was buried where he died, in Susquehanna, Pennsylvania. Soon after Tylea was born, Beatrice had a blood clot in her leg soon and was not able to work, so Dorothy left school after spring vacation when she was sixteen years old to help support the family. She worked five days a week at the Peerless Knitting Mill in Barre for about a year:

I had to walk to work and be to work at 7:00 in the morning, clear down on South Main Street. I tended bobbins all day long and that meant I walked a long ways to tend those bobbins back and forth, back and forth. And then when my day's work was done at 5:00, I walked home. I earned $7.50 a week, and I gave my mother $5.00. (August 29, 1989)

The next year Dorothy worked first at the Washington County Hospital, which was then the sanitarium for tuberculosis, and later at the Theta Chi House at Norwich University. She roomed at each worksite. When the work as a cook at Norwich proved too physically demanding, she returned home to live with her mother and younger brothers and sisters. The family was receiving state support for some of the children at that time, and Beatrice was also taking in foster children in order to help with expenses. Not long after that, Dorothy met John Rogers, the man she was to marry in 1930 at age 20.

MARRIAGE AND FAMILY

John Myron Rogers was thirteen years older than Dorothy. He had dropped out of school in the sixth grade to go to work. He belonged to the carpenter's union and became a skilled craftsman who later operated his own contracting business. When John and Dorothy first married they lived with her mother, Beatrice, in the house on Trow Hill and paid her $3.00 a week for rent. Marion, their first child, was born November 29, 1930. Fifteen months later their second child, Elizabeth (my mother), was born. Dorothy and John later had three more children: Beatrice, John, Jr. and David. Soon after Elizabeth was born they moved to the second floor in the house and paid Beatrice 50 cents a week for electricity and $1.26 a week for milk and other groceries:

I took in washings upstairs. I had $40.00 to buy my furniture and start housekeeping up there. I bought a stove, a nice kitchen stove for ten bucks. I bought two rocking chairs for $2.00 a piece. I bought a library table. And I had my bed. (August 29, 1989)

John rarely ate dinner at home and was gone most of the time working as a carpenter or looking after his mother who lived on Webster Avenue in Barre. To bring in much needed income Dorothy did laundry and dug dandelions:

That got me a little money. And I got the kids a bicycle. I sent away and got Marion and Betty [Elizabeth] two nice bicycles. For some reason I couldn't tell him [John] what I was doing because every time I would say I wanted this or I wanted that the air was always blue. He was always swearing. But when it came to buying the place he had the money to pay for it. He had it buried in the ground. It stunk so, I'm telling you! They put the talcum powder to it—all moldy! (August 29, 1989)

My mother, Elizabeth Rogers Morse, states that as early as she can remember, her mother was taking in laundry:

I can't say that my childhood was happy. I was forced to work when I was very young, and I was forced to earn money to help support the family. Mother always had to work taking in laundry. There was frozen laundry hanging up all over the house all winter. I had to do all the ironing and mangling. Of course, everything was 100% cotton back then. [Mother] took in laundry from five wealthy families in town. My father was working as a contractor. During the depression he lost everything in the banks. (January 29, 1990)

Dorothy also raised chickens and Elizabeth helped with the effort. "When I was in 4-H, I was in an enterprise of raising broilers. I delivered them to the wealthier people in town about the time I was twelve years old." (January 29, 1990)

Christmas during those days was a celebration for the immediate family. Elizabeth remembers hanging up stockings and scurrying to see what was in them. "The stockings were always a disappointment. They filled them with coal and some nuts. There might have been a comb for your hair, not much of anything. There were one or two gifts for each of us under the Christmas tree." (January 29, 1990)

Elizabeth states that her maternal grandmother was the closest adult to her during her youth:

She was a woman of a great deal of love and compassion. She'd give you anything she had. She knitted sweaters and mittens. She worked at the Gary Home in Montpelier for quite a number of years and then she had heart trouble so she had to quit. She died in 1949. (January 28, 1990)

(L. to r.) (Back) Leo Sanborn, Dorothy and John Rogers, Elizabeth holding David; (front) Stuart and Richard Sanborn, Beatrice and Johnny Rogers, Peco (dog), 1944.

eing only fifteen months apart, Marion and Elizabeth were very close sisters. They worked and played together, especially since they were in the same grade in school. Elizabeth remembers when she and Marion wanted to start going to church:

> We asked Mom if we could go to church; she said we could, but it was quite a ways to walk and she would prefer that we went to the church that she knew about which was the Methodist Church. We wanted to go, so she went down to Homer Fitts and bought us each a coat so that we could be warm enough to make the walk to church. It was a mile one way. So we would walk down to the church, just us two girls and we'd go to church. . . . After Marion died, I kept going to church. I joined the church and sang in the choir and was in the youth group. (January 28. 1990)

TURNING POINTS

Significant events occurred in the 1940s which helped to shape Dorothy's adult life and draw her into what was to become an intermittent ministry for her for about twenty-seven years. The first was the death of her eldest daughter and the second was the acquisition of a driver's license. Marion died of a heart condition while playing during recess at the Trow Hill School. She "was twelve years, five months and nineteen days old, and that was 1943 in May." (December 30, 1976) The family was shaken by the death, and John and Dorothy decided to have another child to lessen the focus on their loss.

David was born in 1944 after a very difficult pregnancy. When David was about three months old, Dorothy awakened from a nap one afternoon and "there was a big white cloud and in this cloud

176

was Jesus. And his arms were outstretched. Oh, I just knew this was something wonderful! I searched, I tried to find somebody that could tell me what this meant. [No one] could satisfy the longing in my heart, because I wanted to find God." (December 30, 1976) This was Dorothy's first supernatural experience, the harbinger of a different way of life.

The year 1949 was crucial for Dorothy in terms of liberating experiences. While David was growing up, Dorothy had not driven a car. Elizabeth states that Dorothy enjoyed riding on the back of John's motorcycle when they went out for recreational drives, but that Dorothy relied on John for transportation when the car or truck was needed. (January 29, 1990) Dorothy relates her humorous story of getting her driver's license, a story she enjoys telling:

> When I got the license to drive the car I had to do that unbeknown to John. He got the new car, that was in '49; he had it down there in the garage. And I thought, "Hey, He's worn out all these vehicles; you're a fool, why don't you get a license." So what did I do? I called his niece. I says, "Eunice, would you take me out and see if I'm able to get a license?"
>
> I used to know how to drive, handle a car, but I hadn't since he swore at me something terrible one time over in New Hampshire going through the White Mountains. So I never touched the wheel after that, anyway, she said that she would come and help me. I says, "How many times you think I ought to go out?"
>
> She says, "I think you're all ready."
>
> "Really?"
>
> She says, "Yep."
>
> I had a book and I studied it and do you know I went down in the brown Dodge and I got my license! John was with his truck working somewhere, so I got my license.
>
> The next day I says, "Johnny, would you drive the brown Dodge up here so I can go down and get my teeth taken care of?"
>
> "Oh, no, Dot, nothing like that. If you had a license, it'd be a different story."
>
> I said, "It would?"
>
> He said, "Yes."
>
> I says, "You mean to say if I can produce a license I can drive that car?"
>
> "Yeah."

I walked right into the bedroom and I got my license. I told him how I did it. So I got the car! (August 29, 1989)

It was also in 1949 that Dorothy first began attending church on a regular basis. Her daughter, Beatrice, was dating a young man who attended evangelistic services and Billy Graham crusades. Elizabeth attended some of these services with the couple and later both she and Dorothy attended. It was at one of these services that they met a minister who invited them to visit in his church. (January 28, 1990) Dorothy and her two daughters decided to attend a church service.

Elizabeth explains that the service was different from any she had ever experienced. The church service was participatory with hand clapping, shouting, raising of hands, loud prayer and call and response patterns. There was a strong emphasis on salvation which was grounded in scriptures familiar to Elizabeth. She sensed a different approach to those scriptures in this particular service, however. Elizabeth remembers being somewhat shaken by the service even as she remembers that Dorothy was quite taken with it. Dorothy seemed to find something there which satisfied her. (December 16, 1990) Dorothy recalls:

> We went in and there were only thirteen people, I believe. But there was something about that service, and it was doing something for the longing within me for God. I had picked up a tract in the church, that's a paper with a little salvation message on it, and I was washing this particular day and oh, how I wanted to reach God. And I happened to think of that tract and I picked it up and there was a prayer. I didn't even know how to pray, but there on that tract was a prayer. I learned that prayer two lines at a time until I had that prayer all down so that I could say it. And that prayer just seemed to hit the longing in my very being.
>
> I couldn't hardly wait until it was time to go to bed--I was sleeping upstairs. I got down on my knees that night and I said that prayer. I confessed every known sin, asked the Lord to forgive me of all my sins and I said this prayer, "Oh, Lamb of God, I come. Cleanse me from all my sins in your precious blood. Make me a creature in Yourself. Fill me with your Holy Spirit, I take you now to be my savior and gladly yield my all to Thee. Accept me, oh Lord, and assure me of my acceptance that I may be ready for the coming of the Lord." I got into bed and along in the night there came a touch on the back of both

of my hands. And it was like an electric current going straight through me. I knew something was happening in the spiritual realm; I just was so thankful for it, and I wouldn't say anything to anyone. I could hardly wait to go to bed the next night, got on my knees beside my bed, said this prayer again, and along in the night there came the touch on the back of both my hands again. Twice it happened that night and I'll never forget it. The next night there came a touch on the back of my hand and my right hand went up and the heavens parted. There were the angels worshipping the Lord, and the glory that came down from the throne of God! It was greater than any sunset that I'd ever seen. Wind was coming from every direction and the roar was similar to that of Niagara Falls. It was a tremendous experience. It seemed just like the whole room was vibrating. And I said, "Thank you, Jesus;   thank you, Jesus." And this word came to me, "power," "power." I couldn't get up. All I could do was just lay there the whole night through. It was just glory, wonderful surging, moving, all through my body that whole night.

When I went downstairs that next morning I looked across the breakfast table to my husband and he said, "What in the world has happened to you?"

I told him and the tears rolled down his cheeks. He says, "Don't tell anybody, they'll think you're crazy." (December 30, 1976)

Dorothy had several visions around the time of her salvation experience:

One night I was awakened and I saw a huge Jewish star, all made up of little stars in the heavens. At the same time I saw a huge cross and it was sort of lying down on a slant. That was all made up of beautiful stars. And then another vision I had was the dove. And these came just a few nights apart, all those beautiful visions. And this dove, it was in a circle and this dove in the center, all of beautiful stars.

Another time I saw this big white angel. And it came to me very vividly that it was Gabriel. He was in the midst of a whole lot of people all in black. But he was pure white, his clothing was pure white. And then another vision that I saw, I knelt to pray and the heavens just opened and showed me this old man and he had a sort of sickle-like, and it came to me—Moses or Elijah. (December 30, 1976)

When I asked Dorothy why she thought she had such tangible spiritual experiences she explained:

I believe God Almighty can reveal himself to a heathen in Africa or any other place without anybody ever witnessing to them. He's powerful. Seeing that I didn't know about the Word of God, this is why God had to be so real to me, whereas if someone had been brought up in Sunday School and had always had the Bible taught in their home, God wouldn't have to manifest Himself the way He did. (December 30, 1976)

THE BEGINNING OF A MINISTRY

After her salvation experience, Dorothy began attending the small church in Plainfield, Vermont, where she and her daughters had visited. The acquisition of her driver's license allowed her the freedom to attend church and live a completely different life from her previously restricted lifestyle. (August 29, 1989) She began to read and study the Bible; it was also at this time that she began to have experiences with healings at home and in the community, in church and in the nursing homes around Central Vermont where she worked as a nurse's aid:

> The first time God ever used me in the lines of casting out of a demon was with my own son. I had been up all night with him with an earache. And about seven in the morning I had come to the end of my rope and I started for the phone to call the doctor and on the way to the phone the Spirit of the Lord spoke to me, says, "Go ask him if he believes God will heal him." I went to him and I says, "David, do you believe God could heal you?"
> He said, "Yes."
> I sat down beside him and I laid my hand on his arm. I says, "You say these words after me, David. Dear God, cast out this devil out of my ear in the name of Jesus."
> And as he began to say those words before he got to the name of Jesus he popped like a piece of popcorn from his back right onto his hands and knees and he hollered out,"Mama, He did it! It went ping, it's all gone!" I knew God was able to do things, but somehow you're almost knocked off your feet when you see that God does it. (December 30, 1976)
> In the early 1950s there had been an accident on Trow Hill. A car coming down the hill had gone out of control and pinned two young girls against a building. One of the girls was killed; the other one was injured.
> And the anointing came upon me at that time to go and pray for this girl. Well, I kept putting it off and putting it off. I just started to drive the brown Dodge, that is, I hadn't been driving it very long.

Oftentimes my husband used the car. As I was coming out Elm Street, and this was about the third time the Lord had spoken to me, the anointing came upon me to go and pray for this girl. I had my hands on that steering wheel and [it] just vibrated back and forth. I said, "Yes, Lord, I'll go tonight."

I had quite a time getting the car that night because Mr. Rogers wanted that car. But I said, "I need it, I need it bad." I went over to that place. This girl [the one who was injured] came right over and sat right down beside me. And then I said, "You people probably wonder why I'm here. I believe the Lord has sent me to pray for this girl that has been injured." So I took out the scripture. I read scripture on healing and I says to the stepmother, "Would you like for me to pray for her here or would you like me to go into her room to pray?"

She says, "You can go into her room." And so I went into her bedroom and prayed for that girl and God undertook for her.[2] (December 30, 1976)

During the 1950s the New England annual campmeeting for Assembly of God churches was often held in Plainfield, Vermont. At one of these meetings, Dorothy had her first personal experience with healing during a church service:

All the people that were sick and afflicted were called forward to sit in the front row and be prayed for by different ones. [There] was a man there with a paralyzed hand; it was right down in his lap; he couldn't lift it at all. And I just laid the tips of my fingers on that man's shoulder. When I did, that hand and that arm began to break loose. His arm was going around and around and around all that afternoon in that service. So I know that God can work and does work. (December 30, 1976)

While working at the Don Camp Nursing Home Dorothy had two significant experiences with healing. One time a man was having a heart attack:

He had the oxygen mask on his face and his eyes were almost set. He was thrashing from one side of the bed to the other. I stood there and [the head nurse] went out to call the doctor again to tell him to hurry. I grabbed this man's hand and I said, "Look to Jesus, James, look to Jesus." And God undertook for that man right there. That man was from France and that testimony went all over France. (December 30, 1976)

On another occasion Dorothy was working a private case at the Don Camp Home when one of the nurses experienced difficulty in administering medicine to one of the patients. Dorothy went in and talked with the patient who told her she would take the medicine if the nurse left the room. The patient took the medicine:

> ...and then we walked across the room, back to the bed and she laid down. I started to pull the covers over her and I took hold of both of her hands 'cause I could just feel the current of God on me and in me. I didn't say anything, only just held her hands, and she pulled her hand away and she put her hand up in the air and she said, "Who is that?" She said, "I used to think it was the Blessed Virgin Mary, but now I just don't know."
>
> I said, "It's Jesus." And tears just flowed down that woman's cheeks. She went all over that place telling how Jesus was made very real to her that day. (December 30, 1976)

Word got around town that Dorothy prayed for people and sometimes people experienced healings. One day a man came to the door of the house and asked for prayer:

> He had been given a year to live. I anointed him with oil [and] he left. A short while later he was in the Barre City Hospital in an isolation room and no one was allowed to see him. When I could get in to see him, when they would allow visitors, I went in. And he rose up on his elbow, he could hardly breathe, he says, "Mrs. Rogers, pray for me." I anointed him with oil and prayed for him. About five months later I was at the Washington County Hospital walking down the corridor. I happened to look into this room and I saw this man sitting on the edge of a bed dangling his feet. He says, "you remember the day you came into the hospital to pray for me?"
>
> I said, "Yes."
>
> "Well, " he says, "that night, along in the night, I heard the most wonderful music. And then a cloud appeared and on   this   cloud was Jesus. And the music stopped and he reached down and touched me. He pulled his hand back up, the cloud moved on and then the music came again.
>
> And just about that time a nurse walked into the room and she said, "Why Mr. Pratt, your bed is drenched!"
>
> Everything on his bed was just sopping wet. And she said, "Oh, My! You can get pneumonia in a situation like this. I'll go right out

and get things to dry you all off." She went out to bring back the dry bedding; [when she returned] the bed was bone dry. His bed was bone dry! And that man lived for several years after that. (December 30, 1976)

In 1953 Dorothy began to conduct services in nursing homes. She started in a home in Chelsea:

I used to handle the whole service. I would take along my autoharp and play some songs and the patients would sing a few songs out of the songbook and then I might read a poem and also take the requests to the Lord in prayer. Then I would give forth the Word and if there were patients there that would like to be prayed for, I'd pray for them. (December 27, 1979).

One day Dorothy was playing her autoharp and singing "It Is No Secret What God Can Do," when a nurse came to her service to tell her a woman wished to see her:

So I went in and I says, "You sent for me?"

And she said, "Yes." She says, "I fell and broke several vertebrae in my back in this fall. I can't lift my head over four inches from the flat bed."

I says, "How do you want me to pray?"

"I want to be healed." I took hold of her hand and I prayed for God to undertake.

When I was through praying she began to push the covers off and I said, "What are you going to do?"

She said, "Sit up."

She sat right up straight and then she laid back down and then she sat right up again and whirled and put her feet over the edge of the bed! In comes a nurse with a tray of stuff. She started to shake like a leaf in a breeze and she says, "Oh, this is a miracle! I got to get out of here!" She said, "I knew things were happening in other places, but I never dreamed they were going to happen here." (December 30,1976)

Dorothy says she "always knew the ministry that God had called me for was in the nursing homes, sick people and the aged." She recalls that in 1953 she had gotten a call about a nurse's aid position in a nursing home. She turned it down because it was not what she wanted to do. But "the Lord spoke to me that I could go into this particular nursing home in His name. I said, 'All right, Lord.' I went to the phone and I called and the job was still open for me. So I went and God began to use me in the homes to minister to the people that were really open for the gospel." (December 30,1979) For many years between 1953 and 1970 she worked in nursing homes as well as led services.

In October of 1976 Dorothy and Lillian Pelkey teamed up to do nursing home ministry together. They had met each other at the North Barre Assembly of God Church. "We first started at the Chelsea nursing home; it has just grown ever since." In 1979 they were holding services for about a hundred people a week. "Every Sunday morning at the Rowan Court Nursing Home we take complete charge of the service. [Lillian] plays the accordion; we sing together and pray and we have the message from the Word of God. And then every other Thursday we are in Heaton House. Friday afternoon we are at the McFarland Nursing Home." They also did services for senior citizen groups, were guest singers at churches in Central and Northern Vermont, and ministered in other nursing homes such as St. Jude in South Barre. (December 27, 1979)

Dorothy rarely had notes for her messages. "I just take the Word of God and give it forth, and very few times do I ever have anything written down as to what to say. Most always it seems I can be working around and here comes something right out from somewhere—it comes by the Spirit of the Lord. He lays it on my heart and then I go to the scripture and I begin to search. This is how [the message] gets formulated." (December 27, 1979)

In 1980 Dorothy and Lillian ceased their nursing home ministry after Dorothy broke her shoulder. They had regularly provided services for five years together. All in all, Dorothy had an active nursing home ministry for fifteen years of her life. In speaking of her ministry, Dorothy says, "You're going in there and you're ministering to people who are right on the brink of stepping over into eternity and if they die without Christ they're lost. And if they accept God, they're going to be with the Lord. I feel there isn't a greater ministry done." (December 27, 1979)

In reflecting on Dorothy's religious life and experiences, Elizabeth states, "When she came to the Lord she changed a lot. Her language was terrible before. She was a violent person, didn't have much patience with children. She was under too much pressure to have to work; there was constant financial stress." (January 28, 1990) Dorothy's focus changed from the difficult life she had experienced to a realm of beauty and peace which she realized through her visions and personal connections with the individuals for whom she prayed. Her nursing home ministry became an outlet for her to share her most intimate positive experience with others. "She felt more fulfilled during that period of her life than any other," according to Elizabeth. (January 28, 1990)

WEAVING THE FABRIC

Since I was born after my grandmother, Dorothy, had become involved in church work, I have always known her as a person connected to an Assembly of God congregation. As a small child and up until my junior high school days, I regularly attended the same church with my grandmother. Church was about the only connection we had, for I rarely visited her and my grandfather as I did my paternal grandparents. I remember well the campmeeting times in Plainfield when the men of the region would hoist a huge circus tent where the services were held for two weeks in late summer. The sawdust smell beneath our feet, the cricket call as darkness fell, the burgundy velvet altar cloths soft under our knees as we prayed, are all vivid recollections. I listened intently to the words of the preachers, knew there was something special there amid the emotional fervor of the evening service, but recognized that the experience was perhaps more meaningful for others than it was for me. It was only as I discovered that one's life story has much to do with how one seeks spiritual truths for oneself that I realized I was not rejecting a part of my past when I joined a mainline Protestant church. Those early church and campmeeting experiences connected me with the pain and longing of others' lives, pain and longing which were foreign to me in any other aspect, since my life has not been nearly as difficult as the lives of either my grandmother or mother.

As I reflect on the material within these pages, I find the Christmas stocking narratives especially revealing. My own childhood experiences with stockings were pleasant. I had Dad's faded red cotton sock which I hung on the doorknob to my bedroom door before I went to sleep on Christmas eve. In the morning I awakened to find the stocking bulging with oranges, nuts, candy and inexpensive practical gifts. I listened intently for the reindeer on the roof for as long as I could possibly stay awake, and to this day I know I heard their hooves!

Bicycles play an important part in the memories of all three of us. My grandmother mentioned buying the bicycles for Marion and Elizabeth. At the end of our interview on August 29, 1989, we were discussing her father, when another bicycle story came to mind. She and her brother, John, had desperately wanted a bicycle:

> The only way we could have a bicycle was when my Uncle Beck would throw away an old frame, we might find some old carriage wheels and we'd work at that trying to get those carriage wheels onto that bicycle. Well, we picked strawberries for 2 cents a basket over on the other road. We earned five dollars and Stanley Owens had a bicycle and he said he'd sell it to us for five dollars. We said we wanted it; we brought it home. Oh, we were happy; we had a bicycle and it operated! My father made us take that bicycle back and get that five dollars and when we got home with the five dollars he took it and goes off on a drunk.
>
> And at the time my father died, my brother says, "I wish I could look through his pants pockets to see if I could find five dollars." (August 29, 1989)

My first bicycle was not a new one; it was mother's made over bicycle that my parents repainted and repaired so that it was useable. The balloon tires made it a wonderful bike for jumping ramps and for traveling dirt roads. No one ever made me give my bicycle back.

As I was completing my interviews and preparing my field notes for writing this article, my grandmother, mother and I decided we should visit the cemetery in Barre where my grandmother's ancestors are buried. That experience was memorable. We talked about people and stories long forgotten, shared common memories, and explored the cemetery. Grandmother showed us the iron fence surrounding the upper part of the cemetery. The fence was the result of the work of the Methodist Women, an effort led by my grandmother's great-grandmother.

The depth of sharing between three generations of women which culminates in this article is not measured in these pages, nor can it be. The outcome of oral history work among family members is lived out in the lives of those who made the connections. It is our lives that are enriched. The reader gets only a glimpse of vibrant color and one short brush against the texture of these lives. The fabric is stronger as a result of the oral history process.

Dorothy Rogers (left) and Lillian Pelky, 1978.

CONCLUSION

I have found that collecting oral history from family members poses certain dilemmas for the researcher which are not found in conventional oral history research. The most significant problem lies in lack of distance from the narratives and the persons interviewed. Knowing where to stop looking at history and knowing what to share with the reader is paramount to the success of the research. The fibers of where one life ends and another begins are difficult to distinguish; the researcher must exercise caution. In conventional research the narratives of an interviewee are not connected to the interviewer; they stand by themselves. I found that when a family member relates information involving violence, cruelty and abuse, the subject matter is too close and too uncomfortable for me as well as for the family member telling the story. Since the interviewer knows more details than he or she does in a conventional situation, one never feels that the process of collecting the oral history of a family member is complete. There is always more the researcher knows; there is always more to tell. The interviewer gets caught up in a personal introspective process that diverts his or her attention from the more typical analytical research of the oral historian. It is difficult to avoid bringing emotion-laden extraneous personal introspection into the documentation.

Another dilemma facing the researcher who collects from family members is the surfacing of new questions. As I began writing this article and working through the transcripts, I wondered how much my grandmother's memories of and experiences in her house are connected to the

Dorothy Rogers and Rebecca Morse, Maplewood Cemetery, 1990.

house itself. Does the house just happen to be a place where events occurred and experiences happened, or does it hold special meaning because of its unique history? Is it significant to my grandmother that the house was passed down in the family through a line of women instead of men? What happened that Beatrice, the third daughter in the family, acquired the house instead of the second daughter, who would have likely acquired the house after her older sister had died? Why does my grandmother say that she hopes the house stays in the family when her will states that upon her death the house will be sold and the proceeds from the sale will be divided among the children? Does the house serve as a symbol for Dorothy? The questions continue and continue; the house is just one subject around which an entire set of additional questions are generated. Oral history research conducted with family members is not merely a collection of events and stories but a development of an historical perspective on an individual within the family context. When college students want to collect from family members, they tend to deal first with stories that are told and retold within the family; they also tend to deal with oral history as a collection of memorabilia, not as a continuum of narratives within a specific context. Items are isolated and not treated in a holistic manner. When I first started interviewing my grandmother I was looking for very specific pieces of information, narratives which pertained to particular subjects such as her preaching style or her faith healing experiences. It was only as I pieced the narratives together and researched additional areas of my grandmother's life that the process changed for me. From an emotional standpoint, the task at hand became increasingly difficult. I was dealing with information with which I had no prior contact and I began to see the threads which bind three generations of women together. The interviews involving pregnancy outside of marriage provide a case in point. I had known for many years that my grandmother had been pregnant when she and my grandfather were married; however, I had not known that the same situation was also true for her mother and her grandmother. It was significant, then, that my mother married before becoming pregnant. Through studying the information given me about these pregnancies and the underlying family issues surrounding them, I realized that the only way my mother could know the family pattern was broken was for me to not get pregnant before marriage. Knowing that history certainly helps me to understand my mother's attitude concerning my relationship with boys during the time that I was a teenager.

The trendy past time of collecting family tales is probably harmless and a lot of fun, but the serious oral historian is dealing with something difficult, complex and endless when he or she embarks upon a family research project. I want to ensure that the students I teach understand the difference. The professional researcher should be prepared to deal with topics and issues family members have not discussed openly. The advice I give to students still stands.

NOTES:

1. A mangle is a large roller heatd with electricity; it was used for pressing clothes in the 1930's and 1940's.

2. God "healed" her.

INTERVIEWS

Morse, Elizabeth.   Interview with Rebecca Morse, Calais, Vermont, January 28, 1990.

Morse, Elizabeth.   Telephone conversation with Rose Poulen, Calais, Vermont, June 25, 1990.

Morse, Elizabeth.   Telephone conversation with Rebecca Morse, Calais, Vermont, December 16, 1990.

Morse, Elizabeth and Dorothy Rogers. Conversation with Rebecca Morse, Barre, Vermont, June 26, 1990.

Rogers, Dorothy. Interview with Rebecca Morse, Barre, Vermont, December 25, 1976.

Rogers, Dorothy. Interview with Rebecca Morse, Barre, Vermont, December 30, 1976.

Rogers, Dorothy. Interview with Rebecca Morse, Barre, Vermont, December 27, 1979.

Rogers, Dorothy. Interview with Rebecca Morse, Barre, Vermont, August 29, 1989.

Rogers, Dorothy. Heaton House Service Attended by Rebecca Morse, Montpelier, Vermont, December 27, 1979.

Rogers, Dorothy. Privately published personal tract, 1968.

Visit to Maplewood Cemetery, Barre, Vermont, June 26, 1990.

Rogers, Dorothy. Tape Recording of Heaton House Service, Montpelier, Vermont, August 31, 1978.

****

CONTRIBUTORS

Jane Beck is a folklorist and director of the Vermont Folklife Center in Middlebury, Vermont. She is currently president of the American Folklore Society.

Rebecca Morse, a folklorist, serves as executive director of the Adult Learning Programs of Alaska. She is currently at work on *Telling Stories, Writing Lives: The Alaska Companion,* which incorporates oral history transcriptions and local writing into the teaching of writing in Alaska Adult Education Programs.

Eleanor Ott is a folklorist who for the past twenty years has taught at Goddard College and in the graduate program at Vermont College. Presently she is associated with Foodworks, an educational consulting organization in Montpelier, Vermont.

Jennifer Post, an ethnomusicologist, is Curator of the Helen Hartness Flanders Ballad Collection and of the Vermont Archive of Traditional Music at Middlebury College. She has served as a visiting professor in the Music Department there over the last 12 years.

Gregory Sharrow serves as staff folklorist and director of educational programming at the Vermont Folklife Center.

Dick Sweterlitsch is a folklorist and a member of the English Department at the University of Vermont

DATE DUE
